Walking The Journey

Life with the Lord

Volume 1

ଚ୨ଚ୨ଚ୨ଚ୨

Susan Osborn Schultz

2017 · Gilbert, AZ

WALKING THE JOURNEY: Life with the Lord, Volume 1
By Susan Osborn Schultz
© 2017 by Susan Osborn Schultz
ALL RIGHTS RESERVED.

Published by Susan Osborn Schultz

Mailing Address
Susan Osborn Schultz
P. O. Box 3425
Gilbert, AZ 85299

Internet Addresses
Email: SusanOsbornSchultz@gmail.com
FaceBook: Susan Schultz
Devotional Blog: godswordtowomentoday.blogspot.com

Unless otherwise stated, Scripture references are from the New American Standard Bible.

ISBN 978-1981982417

Printed in the United States of America

❧❧ Endorsements ❧❧

I have known Susan Schultz for a little over five years. She was an Associate Pastor of the Church I pastored for those five years and was a tremendous blessing to me and the church family. Susan has a tremendous heart for people to see them changed by the love and power of God. She is a judicious student of the Word of God and excellent Bible teacher, bringing out truths in God's Word that are simple and yet profound in nature. I have read excerpts from her devotional, *Walking the Journey: Life with the Lord*, and the reader will be blessed, encouraged, and challenged to grow in their relationship with the Lord and come to understand His love in a deeper and more intimate way. Grace and Peace.
David Kibben, Senior Pastor
Family Harvest Church, Cheyenne WY

Motivated by genuine compassion, Pastor Susan Schultz offers us daily doses of comfort and hope that are timeless and relevant. These are profound yet simple examples of how to apply the wisdom found in the Bible. Take the opportunity to experience God's love and be encouraged today! *Rachel Henman, Graduate*
Cheyenne Bible Training Center, Cheyenne, WY

After reading Susan Schultz's devotional, *Walking the Journey, Life with the Lord*, I felt like I had found a friend with whom I could walk through the Scriptures. In her own loving way and with her unique perspective, I found a refreshing, thoughtful, insightful, and uplifting daily devotional and journal, combined in a most useful way. In her heartfelt and well-presented thoughts are found a refreshing stream of life-giving water from the Word of God. This

book can only enhance your own journey of life.
>George M. Stover, D.Min., Th.D., Ph.D., Pastor
>Wellspring Church of All Nations, Las Vegas, NV

Susan's devotionals are Spirit led and very inspirational to my soul. Her writing draws me into God's presence. I always look forward to hearing from God through reading what Susan has written.
>*Ruby Lindblad, Board Member*
>*Northern Colorado Chapter*
>*Christians for Biblical Equality*

The book you are holding in your hands is brimming over with truths and insights from the Word of God. *Walking the Journey* feels like chatting with a close friend. Susan shares her thoughts with the relaxed style of a casual conversation. She has a special gift of taking scripture and drawing out nuggets for you to reflect on all day long. Don't rush through the book, but take your time to mull over the scriptures for yourself. This is a devotional book that you will want to return to again and again as you walk through your own Journey with the Lord.
>*Rhonda Klug, M.Div.*
>*God's Word to the World College, Registrar*
>*God's Word to Women, Inc., Board of Advisors*

I am so honored to be able to write an endorsement for Reverend Susan Schultz. I have known Susan for around thirty years. Not only is she a dear, dear friend, but she has also been the most sold-out, steady Christian I have known.

This book that God called Rev. Susan to write, *Walking The Journey, Life with the Lord*, will literally help you walk your journey. My dear friend, Rev. Susan, has helped many walk their journey and fulfill their destiny. You can be assured, if this is the book you choose for your devotional, that it has been dissected, studied out, and brought to you straight from heaven.

It is a devotional you can be confident in and share with your daughters, granddaughters, grandsons, mothers, grandmothers, friends, sisters, and brothers, to walk their journey and to enlighten them each day as they read it "to walk and live a powerful life with the Lord."

Charlene Baktamarian, Ordained Minister
God's Stations Television Network (GSTN),
Founder/President
God's View Program, Christian Talk Show Host

Susan is a true friend and diligent minister of the Gospel. Tried by fire as she has faithfully followed the Lord Jesus—especially as a woman in ministerial leadership—she is pure gold. You will be enriched and stabilized in your daily walk as you read her experiences and reflect on what each devotional means in your own life.

Dr. Susan Stubbs Hyatt
God's Word to Women, Inc., President/CEO
Int'l Christian Women's Hall of Fame, Founder/Director

Acknowledgements

I want to express thanks to my family whom I love greatly. They have always been my supporters and encouragers as I have followed God's direction for my life.

I want to express my thanks to all those who have invested in my life as wonderful and loving special friends. They have cared enough to challenge me to keep going forward as they faithfully prayed for me.

A special and heartfelt thanks to Rhonda Klug and Sue Hyatt for their dedication and encouragement in bringing about this devotional.

Contents

Introduction   12

Devotional

1. Letting God Love on Me   15
2. God's Love in Us   17
3. Reach Out and Touch Someone   19
4. Sinning Against God's Love   21
5. Mouth Bullies—No Match for God's Love   23
6. It's About Love and Trust   25
7. The Yoke of God's Love   27
8. Sticks and Stones Are Not of Love   29
9. Being Encouraged by Others   31
10. God's Love Is Real   33
11. Four Basic Needs   35
12. Is My Love for God?   37
13. We Are His Favorites   39
14. We Are the Apple of God's Eye   41
15. It's a Comment! Take It or Leave It   43
16. What Is in the Heart?   45

17. Let God Be God   *46*

18. We Are Not Orphans   *48*

19. Being Filled with the Holy Spirit   *50*

20. God Is Worthy   *52*

21. Praise the Lord!   *54*

22. God Dances   *56*

23. Changing on the Inside   *58*

24. Our Walk of Faith   *60*

25. God's Revelation   *62*

26. One Touch, One Word   *64*

27. The Fire Is Burning   *66*

28. Teach Me, Holy Spirit   *68*

29. Loving God's Word   *70*

30. God's Word Is Truth   *72*

31. Just Keep It Simple   *74*

32. Invest in God's Word   *76*

33. Break Up the Fallow Ground   *78*

34. Choose to Think on God's Ways   *79*

35. Empowerment with Word   *81*

36. Be Salt   *84*

37. The Vision   *86*

38. Where Is Jesus When You Need Him?   *88*

39. Be Expectant   *90*

40. Fear of "Hello"   *92*

41. Step on Stepping Stones   *94*

42. God Takes Care of the Lilies   *96*

43. God Rebuilds Ruins   *98*

44. Step into It   *100*

45. We Are in Good Hands   *102*

46. Stop the Pit Bulls. Be Territorial.   *104*

47. Possess Your Land   *107*

48. Why Is This Happening?   *109*

49. Whose Report?   *111*

50. Come   *113*

51. Stir Up the Gifts   *115*

52. Strength in Weariness   *117*

53. Faith Is the Believer's Way of Life   *119*

54. Jesus Is the Answer   *121*

55. Cell Phone   *123*

56. God Has a Good Plan   *125*

57. Joy Testimony   *127*

58. God Is There   *129*

59. See the Tree, Not the Forest   *131*

60. Judge Them Loved   *133*

61. God Gives Grace and Favor   *136*

62. Faith Is for Children   *137*

63. Trees   *139*

64. Bad Attitude Day   *142*

65. God Is Today   *145*

66. Focused, Not Fearful   *147*

67. The Blame Game   *149*

68. Don't Burn Out   *151*

69. When You Don't Want To   *153*

70. Advancing   *155*

71. Forget Not God's Benefits   *157*

72. Touch the Little Ones   *159*

73. God Hears   *161*

74. Be Angry and Sin Not   *163*

75. Teach Me, Lord   *164*

76. Don't Get Bitten Twice   *166*

77. Going with Jesus   *168*

78. Rear-View Mirror Vision   *169*

79. Serving Jesus   *171*

80. God's Wisdom Is in Us   *173*

81. Being Equipped   *175*

82. Stuck in a Rut   *177*

83. Redemption for All   *179*

84. God's Idea   *180*

85. No Teasing   *181*

86. Walk in the Promised Land   *183*

87. Half-Truths and White Lies   *185*

88. What Is the Gospel Truth?   *187*

89. Not Ashamed of the Gospel   *189*

90. Acknowledge God   *191*

About the Author   193

~ Introduction ~

There are so many devotional books, so why another one? I would suggest that the purpose of each of these compilations is to help us know God better and to help us on a very personal level as we journey through life with Him and with each other.

Devotionals, including the ones in this book, are helpful, but they do not replace our personal responsibility to read and study God's Word, The Bible. It is important that we spend quality time reading and studying for ourselves because the Holy Spirit works through the Word of God to change our lives, to set us free, and to bring healing and prosperity. These changes happen as we apply God's Word to our lives.

Starting each new day by meditating on a particular passage, allowing the Holy Spirit to give us inspiring insights helps us keep our focus on the goodness and faithfulness of God throughout the day.

By way of example, five passages are very special to me. They are scriptures that speak of God's call on my life, and I want to show how I have been able to apply them to my life. This is to encourage you.

Nehemiah 8:8. And they read from the book, from the law of God, translating to give the sense so that they understood the reading.

Application: God has given to me the grace and anointing to teach the Word of God in such a way that people can understand and walk in it.

Jeremiah 29:11. "For I know the plans that I have for you," declares the Lord, "plans for welfare and not for calamity to give you a future and a hope."

Application: God has called me to encourage others by letting them know that, no matter who they are and what they have done, God has a great plan for them as they look to Him.

John 8:36. If therefore the Son shall make you free, you shall be free indeed.

Application: God has called me to challenge those who have started in God's Word to continue in it. This is where we find our freedom in Christ Jesus and we will continue in that freedom as we continue in His Word.

Galatians 3:28. There is neither Jew nor Greek, there is neither slave nor free man, there is neither male nor female; for you are all one in Christ Jesus.

Application: The desire of God's heart is to bring release to every born-again individual so that each of us might minister to others. I understand, then, that I am called to speak God's truth in love, while emphasizing that there are no "rejects" or second-class citizens in the Kingdom of God. We are all one—that is, equal—in Christ Jesus, with no respect to nationality, social level, or gender. God has given giftings and callings to each person, and through these we can fulfill His calling on our life, without being hindered by restrictions imposed by human traditions.

2 Timothy 4:16-18. At my first defense no one supported me, but all deserted me; may it not be counted against them. But the Lord stood with me, and strengthened me, in order that through me the proclamation might be fully accomplished, and that all the Gentiles might hear; and I was delivered out of the lion's mouth. [18]The Lord will deliver me from every evil deed, and will bring me safely to His heavenly kingdom; to Him be the glory forever and ever. Amen.

Application: When others come against me as I serve God through His call on my life, Jesus is always there to encourage and strengthen me, especially when others forsake me. Jesus is—and will always be—my unshakable Foundation, and my Stronghold.

So, let me encourage you. God has a call, a direction, a mission, a purpose, and an equipping for every believer, including you. Seek God, and go for it!

1

Letting God Love on Me

> At my first defense no one supported me, but all deserted me; may it not be counted against them. But the Lord stood with me, and strengthened me, in order that through me the proclamation might be fully accomplished, and that all the Gentiles might hear; and I was delivered out of the lion's mouth. The Lord will deliver me from every evil deed, and will bring me safely to His heavenly kingdom; to Him be the glory forever and ever. Amen (2 Timothy 4:16-18).

The Lord gave me 2 Timothy 4:16-18 during a time of persecution from friends whose perception of walking in God's love was different from mine. During this season of walking alone, God gave me some promises that I believe are now coming to pass.

Many people have stood, believing for a turn-around and promises of God to be fulfilled. It may seem like God's promises take forever, but they are always on time. Now is not the time to throw in the towel or give up. With God, things happen suddenly. One thing that we don't have to wait on or stand in faith, waiting for, is the presence of God's love. No matter where we are or what is going on, God's love is with us.

It is knowing, walking in, and experiencing God's love that keeps us on God's path of victory. Today I am going to let God love on me. How about you?

My Reflections   *Date*_____

2

God's Love in Us

Hope does not disappoint, because the love of God has been poured out within our hearts through the Holy Spirit who was given to us (Romans 5:5).

Many years ago, a precious sister in the Lord—she has since gone on to rejoicing with the Lord in Heaven—and I attended a meeting at Barn 13 during Cheyenne Frontier Days. This is where the cowboys, their families, and others would gather each evening for a time of worship, praise, teaching, and ministry. These cowboys and cowgirls talked about how they laid their hands on their horses and prayed over them, as well as on their trailers and other possessions. They shared testimonies of the miracles that God had done for them. It was always a blessing to go to those meetings.

One night, the cowboy who shared hit on a verse I had read many times. But this time, it was different. He spoke about every born-again believer having the love of God—the God-kind of love—IN THEM. As he spoke, it became so real to me. It dawned on me that it was God's plan for every believer to operate in this kind of love. It still is God's plan!

Love is doing whatever we can to bring out the best in others, just as this same best is being developed in us. God's love ("love" as a noun) in us will cause us to love ("love" as a verb) in strength as we step out in faith. As we partake of God's Word, God's love changes us from the inside out.

The cowboy who shared from his heart that evening will never know what a difference he made in my life. But out of his love for God, he let that love flow, telling others of God's great love. This isn't about silly love or sloppy *agape*; it is about the real love of God. It is about God Who Is Love.

My Reflections   *Date*_____

3

Reach Out and Touch Someone

A new commandment I give to you, that you love one another, even as I have loved you, that you also love one another (John 13:34).

When we know we are loved by others—family and friends—we are comforted in our thoughts when we think about those precious people. Even though we are confident of their love, when one of them makes an extra effort to show love toward us, it means so much! This special touch from one of them causes us to experience that love in a greater way.

I was reminded of this through something that one of my brothers would do every night. He would text these words to me: *Love you.* Sometimes he would add a silly comment. I looked forward so much to that text! One night, my phone quit working, so I couldn't receive his text. That evening, I really missed that bit of encouragement.

That little extra expression of love meant so much to me and when it was not available, I really missed it. I know in my heart that my brother loves me, but the extra touch spoke volumes. Is there someone who needs your special touch of love today?

My Reflections *Date*_____

4

Sinning Against God's Love

And we have come to know and have believed the love which God has for us. God is love, and the one who abides in love abides in God, and God abides in him (1 John 4:16).

I was attending a funeral when the officiating minister said something that really got my attention. He talked about being "forgiven for sinning against God's love.

In my early days of being born again, I was constantly asking for prayer that I would know and walk in the fear of the Lord. Those who did not understand this request rebuked me for asking for any kind of fear.

That minister's comment about being forgiven for sinning against God's love opened my understanding to what I really meant. Suddenly, I understood what the fear of the Lord is for me: it is not doing or saying anything contrary to God's love. It is a respect for who God is and what God has given. It is not a fear of breaking a law, but it is that I want to be a God-pleaser and walk in the truth of God's love because I love him.

God forgives us when we come to Him with a repentant heart, but I would rather avoid repentance by always walking in an awareness of His love.

My Reflections Date_____

5

Mouth Bullies Are No Comparison to God's Love

No temptation has overtaken you but such as is common to man; and God is faithful, who will not allow you to be tempted beyond what you are able, but with the temptation will provide the way of escape also, that you may be able to endure it (1 Corinthians 10:13).

I had an interesting day—or perhaps, I should say—a *challenging* day. Someone told me that I really needed to think about retiring from my job because I wouldn't compromise. In my job at the time, it was said that the client is always right and nothing I say or do will ever please them. But that is not how it is with the Lord! I am so grateful! God Almighty is My Heavenly Father, and He loves me, and that same love of lives in me.

We can't change other people and their so-called *freedom of speech*, but we can stay in the presence of God's love and remain at peace. The sad part is that the person who was suggesting that I retire knows that I am a Christian and that I will not compromise my integrity. I love my Heavenly Lord and I look forward, one day, to hearing God's Words, "Well done, good and faithful daughter."

God knows the trials and temptations that we face each day through our job and through other people, but He is faithful. He will provide a way of escape. That way of escape is called *faith and love,* not wishy-washy love, flakey love, or lustful love—but His Great Love. Therefore, today, I will choose to smile, be pleasant, and walk in God's love. Mouth bullies are no match for the love of God!

My Reflections   *Date* _____

∾∾ 6 ∾∾

It's About Love and Trust

Let your character be free from the love of money, being content with what you have; for He Himself has said, "I will never desert you, nor will I ever forsake you" (Hebrews 13:5).

I had a sweet little dog named *Malachi*. He was four or five years old when he was given to me. My precious little Malachi had been abused. He had been kept in a cage that was too small for him, and so he could not grow properly. As a result, he was a bit deformed, and by the time he was given to me, he had lost most of his teeth.

It didn't take long for Malachi to love and trust me. He was confident that I loved him, and he trusted me with all his heart. Because of what he had gone through, he distrusted people and their motives, yet he overcame this distrust in order to love me.

Now why am I telling you this? Like Malachi, bad things may have happened to us. Or maybe bad things are happening now that make us question the love and motives of our Lord God. But God loves us unconditionally. He doesn't like or condone abuse and He doesn't condone or excuse what has or may be happening.

Sometimes new people come into our lives and we

question whether it is safe to trust them—to let them get too close. But we can trust God. He encourages us not to let our faith and trust in His love waver and turn to unbelief and doubt. Our heart can be filled to overflowing with love when we experience the presence, love, and faith of our God because we have complete trust in His love, in His grace, and in His mercy. We can stand confidently because God will never leave nor forsake us.

My Reflections   *Date* _____

୬୧ 7 ୬୧

The Yoke of God's Love

"Come to Me, all who are weary and heavy-laden, and I will give you rest. Take My yoke upon you and learn from Me, for I am gentle and humble in heart, and you will find rest for your souls. For My yoke is easy and My burden is light (Matthew 11:28-30).

The religious leaders of the day were putting the people in heavy bondage to the law—all 613 "fence laws" that they had built around God's Word. These religious leaders believed that if they could get all of the people of Israel to obey the law on the same day that the Savior would come. They were dogmatic leaders without mercy and grace.

But when Jesus came, He set the people free. He gave them rest. He said, "Yoke up with me. I will not weigh you down with works of law which no one can keep. I will lead and guide you into the victorious walk of mercy and grace."

This is the yoke of God's love.

I believe wholeheartedly in studying the Word because of the revelation that comes through God's love made available to us through Jesus. I would much rather be yoked up with Jesus than be in bondage to man's traditions and laws.

Come! Jesus wants to give you rest. You will find that rest in His presence, not in man-made works.

My Reflections   *Date*_____

8

Sticks and Stones Are Not of Love

Love is patient, love is kind, and is not jealous; love does not brag and is not arrogant, does not act unbecomingly; it does not seek its own, is not provoked, does not take into account a wrong suffered, does not rejoice in unrighteousness, but rejoices with the truth; bears all things, believes all things, hopes all things, endures all things. Love never fails; but if there are gifts of prophecy, they will be done away; if there are tongues, they will cease; if there is knowledge, it will be done away (1 Corinthians 13:4-8).

First Corinthians 13:4-8 is God's Word that describes His love. It means being patient. *Patient* love means being able to stand strong on the inside when facing adversity. Love is not only patient; it is also *kind*. It doesn't use degrading, demoralizing teasing, nor does it use vain and empty words. God's love is patient and kind, and this is the kind of love that flows to us and through us.

Words that are not loving can destroy. Words and actions come at us all day long. The old saying, *Sticks and stone may break my bones, but words will never hurt me*, is a lie! Words have the power to crush and destroy a person. This is why we need God's Words.

God's Word in your mouth has the power to move mountains. It brings comfort and healing when it is seasoned with God's love.

How do we use the words, *I love you?* Are they real? Is God's love flowing through those words or have they become another empty saying to fill up space? God is love. God loves each one of us. In Romans 5:5, Paul says that the love of God is in us to flow through us and make a difference in the lives of those around us.

We need to think before we speak, and when we do speak we are to do so out of God's love, not in jealousy, harshness, or hurtfulness, and not with degrading words. Others may come against us, and it is necessary, sometimes, to state difficult facts, but we must always let God's love be our standard. We are to let love be our language.

My Reflections   *Date*_____

9

Being Encouraged by Others

> Take care, brethren, lest there should be in any one of you an evil, unbelieving heart, in falling away from the living God. But encourage one another day after day, as long as it is still called "Today," lest anyone of you be hardened by the deceitfulness of sin (Hebrews 3:12-13).

Good fellowship is a blessing. Recently, my husband and I had lunch with a young and delightful woman of God. Later, we had the privilege of dining with a wonderful couple whose strong, simple faith was so refreshing.

Unfortunately, because we live in a day and hour when we are so busy that we easily become separated from the people that God has brought into our lives—people with whom we are to build relationships so that we can encourage one another in the Word. God didn't create us to be alone, but the world and the demands of life often keep us separated from others, and we become discouraged.

What can we do to minimize this separation? A good beginning is knowing God's Word and His love. Also, allowing God to pour out His love to us through others is a great strength and blessing. It is nice to know others don't need to be aware of the battles that we face, but God will speak through those people to encourage our heart.

God is so faithful, loving, and caring. He is full of grace and mercy, and most importantly, He is real. Let me encourage you to find some people with whom you can fellowship, and let them tell you what God is doing in their lives. It will encourage and inspire you!

My Reflections   *Date* _____

❧❧ 10 ❧❧

God's Love Is Real

"Draw me after you *and* let us run *together*! The king has brought me into his chambers."

"We will rejoice in you and be glad; We will extol your love more than wine. Rightly do they love you" (Song of Solomon 1:4).

Several years ago, I taught through the Song of Solomon. Many understand this to be a romantic love story, but it is so much more. It describes the walk of the believer from the beginning and going forward. It shows that our deepest need is to know God's love for us.

Mentally we can know that Jesus loves us. We can settle it as fact that He went to the Cross, died, and arose again for us. When we are born again, we can know in our heart that Jesus loves us. But even then, we might question that love because of circumstances or because of other people's words and actions. We might question God's ability to love us because we don't see ourselves as God sees us. We might witness God's love poured out on others, and yet, we might feel alone and unloved.

The Holy Spirit is continuously at work in the heart of every one of us who believes, drawing us closer and closer to the Heart of God. God wants us to know His kind of love. God wants us to know who He is, and not just as "somebody upstairs" or as someone to whom we pray—but as someone with whom we can have a personal relationship, a two-way relationship. We are in the Heart of God. Rejoice and be glad! God loves you.

My Reflections　　　　　　*Date*_____

11

Four Basic Needs

But as for me, by Your abundant lovingkindness I will enter Your house, At Your holy temple I will bow in reverence for You (Psalm 5:7).

It is because of God's love for you and me that we draw near to Him. It is because of His love for you and me that we can worship Him in His presence.

In one of his sermons, Pastor David Kibben shared four basic needs we all have. I found them so helpful that I entered them into my phone to remind me to look to the Lord to fulfill these needs in my own life. So often we look to other people to meet these needs—and God can and does work through people—but He is Our Ultimate Source.

Here are the four basic needs:

1. **Acceptance:** Knowing you are individually loved unconditionally.
2. **Identity:** Knowing you are individually significant and special.
3. **Security:** Knowing you are well protected and provided for.
4. **Purpose:** Knowing you have a reason for living.

It is too easy for us humans to look to jobs and other people to meet our needs. We wrongly expect them to be the source of provision for whatever our need. Instead, we should recognize that we entered into relationship with God because of His great love for us and that He is there for us. That great love has never lessened and never will.

My Reflections　　　　　*Date*_____

❧ 12 ❧

Is My Love for God?

> I will lift up my eyes to the mountains; From whence shall my help come? My help comes from the Lord, Who made heaven and earth. He will not allow your foot to slip; He who keeps you will not slumber. Behold, He who keeps Israel will neither slumber nor sleep. The Lord is your keeper; The Lord is your shade on your right hand. The sun will not smite you by day, nor the moon by night. The Lord will protect you from all evil; He will keep your soul. The Lord will guard your going out and your coming in from this time forth and forever (Psalm 121:1-8).

This morning, the Lord was ministering to me about love—both His love and my love. It is the love of God that is for us. It is the love of God that will never quit on us. It is the love of God that protects us. It is the love of God that says we are important, precious, and valuable. God's love never fails.

But what about my love? Is my love for God? Will my love for God never quit? Will my love protect God's goodness by speaking God's Truth? Does my love say to God, "You are important, precious, and valuable to me?" Love can be one-sided, but it is so much better when it flows in both directions! God is for me and I am for God.

My Reflections *Date*_____

❧❧ 13 ❧❧

We Are His Favorites

> Peter fairly exploded with his good news: "It's God's own truth, nothing could be plainer: God plays no favorites! It makes no difference who you are or where you're from—if you want God and are ready to do as he says, the door is open (Acts 10:34-35, Paraphrased by *The Message Bible*).

It is important to get into the Word and into God's presence each morning. Doing so will set your heart, your focus, and your attitude for the day. I have often shared how my own attitude has changed during certain situations. When I share my experiences, it is to encourage others. It is to say that what God has done for me and in me, He will do for others. God is not a respecter of persons.

For a long time, I have been telling myself and others that I am God's favorite daughter. And it is true because we are all God's favorite daughters and sons. God loves each of us so much that Jesus died and rose again so we can have this very special relationship between Him and us. My confessing this brings the awareness of God's love for me to a personal level.

Until we know that God loves us as individuals, our sense of freedom and relationship with Him is not all that it is meant to be.

Too many Believers seem to have the attitude, "I am just a blob under a blood covering." But that is not how Our Creator sees us!

Both individually and corporately, we are God's favorites, and He enjoys spending time with each of us, His special and unique creations.

My Reflections   *Date*_____

14

We Are The Apple of God's Eye

The righteous cry, and the Lord hears and delivers them out of all their troubles. The Lord is near to the brokenhearted and saves those who are crushed in spirit. Many are the afflictions of the righteous. But the Lord delivers him out of them all (Psalm 34:17-19).

In my life I have gone through the loss of five homes: two by fire, one by tornado, and two by financial losses. None of these losses were God's choosing, yet they happened.

We have an enemy whose intent it is to steal, kill, and destroy our faith in God and His Word through circumstances. The enemy tries to overwhelm us and get us to put our focus on the negative. He tries to steal our hope, kill our successes, and destroy our walk. More importantly, because we are the apple of God's eye, the enemy wants us to question God's love. God's promise to us is that we can trust Him to get us to victory.

My Reflections   *Date*_____

৺৺ 15 ৺৺

It's a Comment!
Take It or Leave It

Finally, brethren, whatever is true, whatever is honorable, whatever is right, whatever is pure, whatever is lovely, whatever is of good repute, if there is any excellence and if anything worthy of praise, let your mind dwell on these things. The things you have learned and received and heard and seen in me, practice these things; and the God of peace shall be with you (Philippians 4:8-9).

One day a woman came into my place of employment and proceeded to critique my hair style. Her opinion was that it made me look old. As I thought about her comments, I wondered how many people try to speak their thoughts into our lives and try to make us see things their way. That is one of the reasons we need to surround ourselves with people we can trust to speak the things of God, His ways, and His truth into our lives.

This woman had a traditional way of thinking, a way that follows man-made doctrines and interpretations of the scriptures. As a result, she walked in great bondage instead of in the freedom found in God's truth. She did not mean to insult me, but she felt free to state her opinion and to assume that I needed to know what she thought. Hmmm? I guess my question is, "What would God's love do?" Now, I can accept her comment or I can file it in *File 13*.

When someone gives us their opinion, as this woman did, we need to look at it through the eyes and heart of God's Word. I love this person, but I know this is not someone whom I would allow to speak into my life about spiritual things. As the saying goes, "We need to eat the hay but spit out the sticks." Then, we need to go a step further and let love burn the sticks!

My Reflections *Date*_____

≫ 16 ≪

What Is in the Heart?

The word of the LORD came to Jonah the son of Amittai saying, "Arise, go to Nineveh the great city and cry against it, for their wickedness has come up before Me" (Jonah 1:1-2).

Jonah was an Old Testament prophet who was sent to reach a group of people for whom he had no love. He believed it was wrong for God to reach out to them. But after a major trial, he did what was required, but his heart was still not in line with God's heart. He feared God, yet he was disappointed when God saved this city full of people.

When we see others—those who are ungodly—being blessed and turning their lives around, even at our expense, what will God find in our heart? His love?

My Reflections   *Date*_____

17

Let God Be God

Rejoice in the Lord always; again I will say, rejoice! (Philippians 4:4).

This is the day the Lord has made. I WILL rejoice in it and be glad. I have had several people ask me why we believers go through so much "stuff." I don't know the answer. I don't know why some people who are doing all they know to do are still fighting major battles. However, we live in a fallen world that is full of "bad stuff."

What I do know is that God is God. God is greater than any situation, and in spite of our situation, God is worthy to be praised and worshipped with all of our heart, mind, and being.

I know what it is like to be wiped out to nothing more than once, to see my loved ones suffer unmercifully, and even to suffer personally. I know what it is like to be rejected by others, persecuted because of my walk with God, and I know what it is like to feel that I am all alone. I have compassion for the pain of others. It breaks my heart.

This one thing I do know, no matter what: God is still God. And because we are His children, God's heart is for us. He loves us, and we never need to question that love. So, whatever we are going through today or tomorrow, let's not ask about all the "whys," but let's put attention—heart, mind, and body—on Jesus, allowing the Holy Spirit to comfort us, letting God be God in our lives!

My Reflections   *Date*_____

❧❧ 18 ❧❧

We Are Not Orphans

Many are the afflictions of the righteous; But the Lord delivers him out of them all (Psalm 34:19).

Many are the afflictions of the righteous, but God delivers!! Wow! What a promise Our Awesome God has given us!

Sometimes it seems as if life is a never-ending series of battles. Hardly is one battle over when another one begins! At such times, do our hearts have confidence in God's promises, confidence in knowing that God will never fail us? God will never leave us nor forsake us! We are not orphans. God will never quit on us and we need never quit on God. God calls us to walk in victory.

God's Word of praise and thanksgiving is a powerful weapon in these battles. This weapon coming out of our heart and mouth, and we speak in faith against the enemy. In ourselves, apart from God's help and intervention, we cannot expect to win. God said the battle is not ours, but His!

We must operate in the God-kind of faith which is based in God's Word, the Bible. We do this by lifting our hands in praise, singing songs of thanksgiving to God. We don't win by being moved by what our physical eyes see or by what our physical ears hear. We win by trusting God to do what He has promised!

My Reflections   *Date*_____

19

Being Filled with the Holy Spirit

So then do not be foolish, but understand what the will of the Lord is. And do not get drunk with wine, for that is dissipation, but be filled with the Spirit, speaking to one another in Psalms and hymns and spiritual songs, singing and making melody with your heart to the Lord; always giving thanks for all things in the name of our Lord Jesus Christ to God, even the Father (Ephesians 5:17-20).

The will of God is written in God's Word, and His will is something we are continually seeking to know in order that we might walk in it. In this passage, we are instructed not to be drunk with wine, but instead, to be filled with the Holy Spirit. The word *filled* means "to fill and keep being filled."

One dose of the Holy Spirit is not enough. People who get drunk in the natural are the ones who are consuming one drink after another. They don't stop with one or two drinks. It's an ongoing process.

As these people continue to drink, they don't seem to care what others think or say. Sometimes you will find them singing, albeit, terribly off key! As far as they are concerned, they are having "fun."

But for those of us who believe, Paul is making it clear that we are to maximize life by being filled to overflowing with the Holy Spirit, not just once, but continuously. That is when we are truly free to sing, dance, praise, and give thanks to God. When we Christians are together and overflowing with the Holy Spirit, we know how to have *a hallelujah time.* That togetherness is such energizing, life-giving, and relationship-building fun! So, don't get drunk on wine—the headache is not worth it! —but instead, be being filled continuously with the Holy Spirit.

My Reflections   *Date*_____

20

God Is Worthy

God be gracious to us and bless us, and cause His face to shine upon us—*Selah*. That Your way may be known on the earth, Your salvation among all nations. Let the peoples praise You, O God; Let all the peoples praise You. Let the nations be glad and sing for joy; For You will judge the peoples with uprightness and guide the nations on the earth. Selah. Let the peoples praise You, O God; Let all the peoples praise You. The earth has yielded its produce; God, our God, blesses us. God blesses us, that all the ends of the earth may fear Him (Psalm 67:1-7).

God is so good to us! God is so worthy of our praise! Although God loves to bless us, He does not become our *Sugar Daddy*. God is the One Who created us for His Glory. God is the One Who created us to be worshippers of Him. Because He created us to be able to worship, it is our nature to worship something or someone, but our worship is to be of God alone.

God is continuously pouring out His love on us. As we worship and praise Him, we feel that love in a deep and intimate way. Oh, what a great day to sing, shout, dance, or kneel before the Lord Our God! What a great day to tell the Lord how much we love Him! God is worthy!

My Reflections   *Date*_____

~~ 21 ~~

Praise the Lord!

Praise the Lord! Praise God in His sanctuary; Praise Him in His mighty expanse. Praise Him for His mighty deeds; Praise Him according to His excellent greatness. Praise Him with trumpet sound; Praise Him with harp and lyre. Praise Him with timbral and dancing; Praise Him with stringed instruments and pipe. Praise Him with loud cymbals; Praise Him with resounding cymbals. Let everything that has breath praise the Lord. Praise the Lord! (Psalm 150:1-6).

Praise God! Everywhere we are, we can praise God, whether it be in a church service or not. We can praise Him on the job, in the field, or wherever our walk takes us.

Psalm 150:1-6 speaks of praising God with music. I find it helpful to play a Christian CD or radio station as an aid in praise.

I like to praise God in my car as I am driving down the road. When I was an associate pastor at a church almost 40 miles from home, I would usually make the return trip three times a week. Rather than being a burden, it was a special time for fellowship with the Lord and it gave me precious time to praise Him.

We may not feel like praising God, or we may not even want to offer praise. But if we will just do it, it will bring us out of the mulligrubs. It brings us into a place of worship of God, Who loves us so much. It fills us with God's peace because our focus is on the Lord. Take time to praise the Lord. It is one of the most important things we can do today.

My Reflections   *Date*_____

◈◈ 22 ◈◈

God Dances

Shout for joy, O daughter of Zion! Shout in triumph, O Israel! Rejoice and exult with all your heart, O daughter of Jerusalem! The Lord has taken away His judgments against you, He has cleared away your enemies. The King of Israel, the Lord, is in your midst; You will fear disaster no more. In that day it will be said to Jerusalem: "Do not be afraid, O Zion; Do not let your hands fall limp. "The Lord your God is in your midst, A victorious warrior. He will exult over you with joy, He will be quiet in His love, He will rejoice over you with shouts of joy (Zephaniah 3:14-17).

This passage describes a lot of activity. Shouting. Rejoicing. Dancing. Singing. All of this because they knew that Almighty God was in their midst!

God wasn't far away. He was right there in the midst of His people. In fact, God was participating in the celebration of worship and praise.

In verse 17, the word *rejoice* means "to spin about under the influence of a violent emotion." That emotion is God's love. God may have done some of the *Charismatic two steps* or the *Charismatic bunny hop* that we see happening today among some of God's people. The picture this passage gives us is of God spinning around! In other words, the entirety of God's Being was involved. God was giving all.

In verse 16, God is telling you to raise our hands. You might say, "Get arrested and celebrate. Don't let your hands hang down in defeat and discouragement."

God has already won the battle, so celebrate with a heart of joy that comes out as you focus on Jesus. By an act of your will, praise God. It will strengthen that tired body, refresh your soul, and set your spirit on fire. God's prescription for weariness is to lift up those hands and spin about under the influence of a violent emotion, your love for God!

My Reflections *Date*_____

23

Changing on the Inside

All Scripture is inspired by God and is profitable for teaching, for reproof, for correction, for training in righteousness; that the man of God may be adequate, equipped for every good work (2 Timothy 3:16-17).

Did you know the Gospel records (Matthew, Mark, Luke, and John) center on the final three and a half years of Jesus' life? They were written to help us to know the Lord and to walk in His ways. They were written to help make our faith strong and powerful. They were written to help multiply God's love in the earth as we reach others with the Good News.

If you haven't already done so, it is time to make a commitment to read God's Word each day. Start by reading just one chapter or by following a reading plan that takes you through the Bible in one year. You can even start by reading just a few verses.

Even when you are not aware of it, and things don't seem to be changing on the outside, they are changing on the inside. That is exactly where it needs to begin!

My Reflections   *Date*_____

24

Our Walk of Faith

Thy word is a lamp to my feet, and a light to my path (Psalm 119:105).

God's Word is a lamp to our feet, lighting our path. In Bible days, travel could be very dangerous, especially at night, and the traveler had to be able to see the path. To help, a night traveler would tie oil lamps onto his feet, and this way he could see the next step. The light on his path helped to protect him from stepping in a hole, falling over the side of a cliff, stepping on a snake, or avoiding anything else that might hinder or stop him. Even with the lamp, the traveler had to pay close attention to his steps. He couldn't see the whole path, but he could see the next step.

Walking in faith is often like walking that path. We know the direction we need to go, but we feel in the dark regarding how to get there. But God's Word will lead, and the Holy Spirit will direct our steps.

Our part is to take the step of faith where God has lighted the path and so advance, one step at a time. Sometimes that first step can be the hardest. But once the commitment and dedication to follow God and His ways are settled, we already have the light to begin walking the path of faith. And so, we will get to our destination victoriously!

My Reflections   *Date*_____

෯෯ 25 ෯෯

God's Revelation

... that the God of our Lord Jesus Christ, the Father of glory, may give to you a spirit of wisdom and of revelation in the knowledge of Him (Ephesians 1:17).

This prayer asks God to give to us a spirit of wisdom and revelation in the knowledge of God. *Revelation* is something known but was not previously realized. Many have a working knowledge of the Bible but lack revelation. In other words, the written word *(i.e., logos)* becomes revelation as it comes alive to us *(i.e., rhema)*.

Studying the Word is important and spending time in the presence of Our Heavenly Father will produce *rhema*. It is *the rhema Word* that activates faith and active faith precipitates results. No matter how hard it may seem, the effort we put into studying the Word of God is worth it. Even when it seems that our prayer time and worship aren't going anywhere, God is still working on the inside, bringing forth revelation of who Our Lord and Savior is and increasing our understanding of how great is the love of Almighty God for us.

My Reflections Date_____

ಅಶಿ 26 ಅಶಿ

One Touch, One Word

He entered again into a synagogue; and a man was there whose hand was withered. They were watching Him to see if He would heal him on the Sabbath, so that they might accuse Him. He said to the man with the withered hand, "Get up and come forward!" And He said to them, "Is it lawful to do good or to do harm on the Sabbath, to save a life or to kill?" But they kept silent. After looking around at them with anger, grieved at their hardness of heart, He said to the man, "Stretch out your hand." And he stretched it out, and his hand was restored (Mark 3:1-5).

Jesus entered the synagogue to bring healing to a man whose hand was withered, hindering him from being whole and doing things that needed to be done. This person could not stretch out his own hand.

On this particular day, Jesus went looking for him. Perhaps only Jesus knew what was about to happen. The man may not have known that Jesus could heal him, and the religious leaders were upset to think that Jesus dared to heal him on the Sabbath.

Imagine what happened in the heart of the one who was healed! One touch, one word from Jesus changed his life forever! And He can do the same for you.

Today, that one word or that one touch can come

through you and me as we listen and obey the leading of the Holy Spirit.

On one occasion, as I was praising and thanking the Lord, He ministered to me that while it is important for us to study and have a good biblical foundation, we must also *believe* the Word. God showed me how He wants the Word to flow out of us to touch those with *the withered hands*—those who have been paralyzed by traditions, and those who have been handicapped because of religious rules and doctrines, and those who have been unable to fulfill God's plan for their lives. Jesus came to set us free. Jesus wants to use us to be His vessels to set others free!

My Reflections　　　　　*Date*_____

27

The Fire Is Burning

At my first defense no one supported me, but all deserted me; may it not be counted against them. But the Lord stood with me and strengthened me, so that through me the proclamation might be fully accomplished, and that all the Gentiles might hear; and I was rescued out of the lion's mouth. The Lord will rescue me from every evil deed, and will bring me safely to His heavenly kingdom; to Him be the glory forever and ever. Amen (2 Timothy 4:16-18).

"Am I okay? I don't have the fire I once had." I have been hearing this a lot lately.

To keep the fire burning, we must stay close to Jesus.

As I thought with the Lord about all of this, I believe He gave me the following understanding. A fire that is bright and hot will burn up its supply of wood quickly and begin to lose power, but a fire that is burning moderately will keep putting out heat longer with enduring power. Being steady and staying in the Word of God will keep us on fire and anointed to bring the warmth of God's love to others.

God gave me the scripture above when I was going through some really hard times. People I had loved and trusted had turned on me and I felt all alone. When this sort of thing happens to us, we don't feel that there is much fire left in us, but God is faithful to keep fueling us with the ingredient called *God's love*.

This morning as I read this passage again, one verse *jumped out* as if I had never read it before! *The Lord will rescue me from every evil deed, and will bring me safely to His heavenly kingdom; to Him be the glory forever and ever. Amen (vs. 18).*

When the fire seems to be burning low, God will take us through—but not just *through that situation*. God will take us all the way through to His Kingdom where there is peace and joy. God is faithful. We can trust Him in spite of what our mind and emotions are telling us. God's Word never fails, and His mercies are new every morning. We can trust Him when our world is turned upside down and we don't feel very *Christian-like*. God will keep the fire burning in us. Jesus is Lord in our lives and over our lives.

My Reflections   *Date*_____

28

Teach Me, Holy Spirit

But when He, the Spirit of truth, comes, He will guide you into all the truth; for He will not speak on His own initiative, but whatever He hears, He will speak; and He will disclose to you what is to come. (John 16:13).

A statement I have written in my Bible is this:

> You are convicted of either what the Word of God says or what your traditions teach you.

The Holy Spirit is such a vital part of our lives. Jesus sent Him to dwell within us so that we can have a living, liberating relationship with God and not be bound up by the demands of mankind's traditions.

The Word of God has power. As we yield to it, we do not give into the pressures of traditions that rob us of wisdom and knowledge from the Holy Spirit that tell us who we are in Christ Jesus and our relationship with Him.

I know I have said this over and over, but one more time won't hurt: *Get into God's Word.* Get a Greek and Hebrew dictionary and uncover for yourself the meanings of key words. Yes! I know the *Webster Dictionary* is good, but going back to the roots is better. Look into the history and culture of the Biblical setting of the passages you are reading. It is exciting what one might find!

Most importantly pray as you are reading, asking the Holy Spirit to show you what His Word really is saying—what is true. Sometimes traditions cloud our understanding, but the Holy Spirit in you wants you to see God's truth clearly and to walk victoriously in it.

Teach me God's truth, Holy Spirit!

My Reflections   *Date*_____

❧❧ 29 ❧❧

Loving God's Word

O how I love Your law! It is my meditation all the day. Your commandments make me wiser than my enemies, For they are ever mine. I have more insight than all my teachers, For Your testimonies are my meditation. I understand more than the aged, Because I have observed Your precepts. I have restrained my feet from every evil way, That I may keep Your word. I have not turned aside from Your ordinances, For You Yourself have taught me. How sweet are Your words to my taste! Yes, sweeter than honey to my mouth! From Your precepts I get understanding; Therefore I hate every false way (Psalm 119:97-104).

Oh, how I love the Word of God!

In it is the wisdom and revelation that I need for my daily walk.

In it is power to change a person from the inside out.

In it is God's Holy Spirit to produce God's fruit of love in the heart of a believer, and from that love will come the desire to follow God's precepts so that we are always pleasing to Our Lord God Almighty.

In it we will grow in the fear of the Lord. *The fear of the Lord* is to be so aware of—so in awe of—and so overwhelmed by the holiness and righteousness of God that it overtakes us.

God's Word humbles us and causes life changes because of *love*—both ours *and* God's. We talk about love all day long. We say, "I love this", or "I love that," loosely using a powerful word. But when we experience the real love of God, we are made aware that this is *real* love—not *sloppy agape*—and because we are so in awe, we have a hard time expressing in words the love we feel!

Thank you for Your Word, Lord, and thank you that we can know You more and more and walk as You have created us to in Your love and expressing Your love.

My Reflections   *Date*_____

❦❦ 30 ❦❦

God's Word Is Truth

The words of the Lord are pure words; As silver tried in a furnace on the earth, refined seven times. You, O Lord, will keep them; You will preserve him from this generation forever. The wicked strut about on every side when vileness is exalted among the sons of men (Psalm 12:6-8).

Psalm 12:6-8, in a paraphrase called *The Message*, says it this way: *God's words are pure words, pure silver words refined seven times in the fires of his word-kiln, pure on earth as well as in heaven. God, keep us safe from their lies, from the wicked who stalk us with lies, from the wicked who collect honors for their wonderful lies.*

God's Word is Truth. God's Word is full of His promises. His Words are healing and create prosperity. God's Word brings freedom and restoration for all who call upon the Name of Jesus and make Him *Lord*.

When I first read this passage this morning, I thought of all the ugliness that is happening in the world. Then, in my heart, I felt the Holy Spirit prompting me to understand that the lies of manmade traditions that are not in line with God's Word are bad because they blind people from seeing God's Truth.

I pray this morning for our eyes to be open to God's truth and for us to be kept safe from the lies the enemy uses to keep people in bondage, especially in the religious world.

My Reflections　　　　　*Date*_____

৵৵ 31 ৵৵

Just Keep It Simple

I solemnly charge you in the presence of God and of Christ Jesus, who is to judge the living and the dead, and by His appearing and His kingdom: preach the word; be ready in season and out of season; reprove, rebuke, exhort, with great patience and instruction (2 Timothy 4:1-2).

The Message paraphrased version reads: I can't impress this on you too strongly. God is looking over your shoulder. Christ himself is the Judge, with the final say on everyone, living and dead. He is about to break into the open with his rule, so proclaim the Message with intensity; keep on your watch. Challenge, warn, and urge your people. Don't ever quit. Just keep it simple.

The Lord spoke this verse to my heart many years ago. No matter where I was or what I was doing, I needed to be willing always to minister God's Word. *The Message Bible* brings it out more plainly.

Now, I have usually thought that I was prepared to preach if called upon at a moment's notice. My humble, but prideful, attitude had been that I never wanted to embarrass My Lord by not being prepared. So, I would carry with me some teachings I had prepared and done in the past whenever I traveled. I spend many hours, carefully preparing messages.

The Lord ministered this verse to me today. He impressed upon me that, as ministers of His Word, we are to share *in season* or *out of season,* that is, when we are called upon suddenly. In such cases, when the Word is in my heart, it will flow. We can't give what we don't have. That is why it is so important for us to get into God's Word, and that is why we need to encourage others to do the same. Not everyone is going to speak publicly, but everyone has opportunities to share God's message from their heart.

My Reflections　　　　　　*Date* _____

≪ 32 ≫

Invest in God's Word

And He said to them, "Rightly did Isaiah prophesy of you hypocrites, as it is written:
> 'THIS PEOPLE HONORS ME WITH THEIR LIPS,
> BUT THEIR HEART IS FAR AWAY FROM ME.
> 'BUT IN VAIN DO THEY WORSHIP ME,
> TEACHING AS DOCTRINES THE PRECEPTS OF MEN.'

Neglecting the commandment of God, you hold to the tradition of men" (Mark 7:6-8).

The other day I was trying to style my hair to make it look nice. I worked at it, and finally, I had it done but then I put on my glasses! To say the least, it needed a lot more work! This is what traditions have done when it comes to seeing the truth of God's Word.

So many people have accepted teachings presented by others. These teachings *appear* to be okay until they "put on their glasses" and get into the Word of God for themselves. Things look different then. The flaws in what they have believed become evident.

This is what happens when they take the time to study and look up words in Greek and Hebrew, learn about the culture of the times, and discover to whom and why God was addressing a message through Paul and other writers.

This kind of study helps us see God's truth clearly. And when this happens, God's Word liberates us from the bondage of traditional teaching that does not declare the truth.

A lot of good and wonderful people are ministering the Word of God, but it is our personal responsibility to invest in God's Word ourselves by studying, praying, and seeking God. As we continue in God's Word, receiving the truth it presents, we experience the liberty Jesus promised.

My Reflections　　　　　*Date*_____

33

Break Up the Fallow Ground

Sow with a view to righteousness. Reap in accordance with kindness; Break up your fallow ground, For it is time to seek the Lord Until He comes to rain righteousness on you (Hosea 10:12).

It is important that we stay focused on God's truth, and live in God's love. This means choosing to give up unforgiveness, offenses, or anything else that would come between God and us. We break up the hard, *fallow ground* of our heart by staying in the Word, and spending time in prayer, praise, worship, and thanksgiving.

My Reflections   *Date*_____

34

Choose to Think on God's Ways

> Finally, brethren, whatever is true, whatever is honorable, whatever is right, whatever is pure, whatever is lovely, whatever is of good repute, if there is any excellence and if anything worthy of praise, dwell on these things. The things you have learned and received and heard and seen in me, practice these things, and the God of peace will be with you (Philippians 4:8-9).

This morning my mind was flooded with negative, past realities. To stay in God's peace, I had to choose not to think those negative thoughts. My experience was not unique. We all have had bad experiences that hurt and wound us. But how we deal with them determines the quality of our life!

In Hebrews 10:30, God tells us that vengeance is His, not ours. When we have been wronged, we are not to retaliate. God will take care of things!

Our well-being comes from thinking and meditating on God's Word, not on our hurts or wounds. Romans 12:2 tell us that the Word will change us from the inside out. So, let's not carry a burden we were never equipped to carry!

My Reflections   *Date*_____

✿✿ 35 ✿✿

Empowerment with Word

> Therefore be imitators of God, as beloved children; and walk in love, just as Christ also loved you, and gave Himself up for us, an offering and a sacrifice to God as a fragrant aroma. But do not let immorality or any impurity or greed even be named among you, as is proper among saints; and there must be no filthiness and silly talk, or coarse jesting, which are not fitting, but rather giving of thanks (Ephesians 5:1-4).

There is a gentleman who has said to me several times, "I thank God for your life." The first time I heard him say it, I had to ask, "What did you say?" Never before had I been told that someone was thanking God for my life!

Yes, I would hear "I am praying for you," and that is so very greatly appreciated. But what hit me about this gentleman's remark was his acceptance of who God had created me to be and the reality of God living through my life. He does not know the power of God that was released through him to encourage me and increase my self-confidence.

Now, there is another gentleman who speaks the opposite in an ungodly manner. When he saw me wearing a nice yellow pant suit that I had just purchased, he announced loudly that I looked like a banana running around. I never wore it again! But he explained his remarks, saying, "Well if I didn't tease her she wouldn't know I loved her!" This is a statement this person uses, thinking he is doing good, but I find no encouragement in it. In fact, his words are destructive.

Both men are good Christians, yet their words created very different results. While one edified the object of his remarks; the other demoralized the person who was the object of his remarks. Teasing, such as what the second gentleman said, has the effect of putting someone down while making the one teasing feel empowered because, through his teasing, he makes people laugh. This is a negative practice!

God spoke His Words to us to empower, encourage, and edify. The first gentleman is an example of being an imitator of Christ; the second one, not so!

Our words are so powerful. They can build up, bring confidence and acceptance, or they can tear down, destroy self-confidence, and minister rejection. So, before we speak, we need to think about what results we are seeking to create with our words. Do we want to only empower ourselves or do we want to be like Jesus and empower others?

My Reflections   *Date*_____

☙ 36 ❧

Be Salt

"You are the salt of the earth; but if the salt has become tasteless, how will it be made salty again? It is good for nothing anymore, except to be thrown out and trampled underfoot by men" (Matthew 5:13).

We believers are called to be the salt of the earth. Salt is used to flavor food, preserve items from spoiling, and destroy the ability of things to grow. Salt is used on food to improve its flavor and thereby increase the eating pleasure of the partaker.

One day, I stopped on my way home to get some sweet potato fries for supper. As I headed home, I had to try one. It tasted bland. It had no salt! But what I didn't know was that there was salt in the bag. I had the salt all the time! As believers we are salt shakers with the ability to add God's flavor to the lives of others.

The salt is the Word hidden inside of our heart. We are here to make a difference. Our words can bring Godly change, as we sprinkle the salt that is needed for the situation. Wisdom helps us know how much salt to sprinkle and when to stop. As *people of salt*, let's improve the lives of those around us, sprinkling God's Word to preserve the good and destroy the work of the enemy. Then we are truly being the salt of the earth!

My Reflections   *Date*_____

37

The Vision

Where there is no vision, the people are unrestrained. But happy is he who keeps the law (Proverbs 29:18).

The word *vision* in this verse can also be understood to mean, "Where there is no revelation of God's truth, the people go anyway they want." In the Book of Judges, the people did that several times. They would go their own way and then cry out to God for help. The people had no vision of God and didn't know His love for them.

I love the old wooden and metal windmills, so one day, I tried to photograph some. But I was not wearing proper shoes—steel-toed to keep from stubbing my toes and knee-high to protect from bites by creepy critters. I couldn't get close and my camera couldn't take close ups.

I could envision my desired results—a picture of a beautiful windmill set against a glorious sunset. In other words, I had a vision for it, but I had not taken time to prepare with what was necessary to bring my vision to pass.

Preparation to achieve our vision in life begins in the Word of God. It is getting the Word instilled in our heart and walking in it that brings our vision to pass.

My Reflections　　　　　*Date*_____

৽৽ 38 ৽৽

Where Is Jesus When You Need Him?

> Do not fret because of evildoers, be not envious toward wrongdoers. For they will wither quickly like the grass, and fade like the green herb. Trust in the Lord, and do good; dwell in the land and cultivate faithfulness. Delight yourself in the Lord; And He will give you the desires of your heart. Commit your way to the Lord, trust also in Him, and He will do it. And He will bring forth your righteousness as the light, and your judgment as the noonday (Psalm 37:1-6).

Comments such as "Where are the cops when I need them?" or "Where is so-and-so when I need help?" or "There is never anyone around when I need help!" are spoken in frustration because of our circumstances. Someone runs a light and nearly hits us! Someone promises to be there and doesn't show up or is late! Even a simple task like trying to open a jar can elicit comments like this.

Circumstances like this interrupt our schedule, disrupt our plans, and upset our expectations. They add new information—good or bad—to what is happening. Such circumstances can rule us or we can rule them. It all depends on your focus.

One thing is sure: Jesus will never leave you. He is The One protecting you from the reckless driver. He is always on time and is never late in encouraging you, helping you, and giving you direction. He is The One who will give you the added strength or the tool to open that jar, or He will send someone to open it for you. So, where is Jesus when you need Him? Right there with you!

My Reflections   *Date*_____

39

Be Expectant

Yet those who wait for the Lord will gain new strength; They will mount up with wings like eagles. They will run and not get tired. They will walk and not become weary (Isaiah 40:31).

Those who wait on the Lord will gain new strength. *To wait* means "to bind together and to tarry in expectancy." Expecting what? Strength.

In place of weakness, God makes a divine exchange. He gives those who seek Him strength in all areas: spiritually, mentally, and physically.

So many people are fighting to stay strong in the storms of life and amid insurmountable circumstances. Sickness, financial lack, troubled relationships, and devastating acts of nature, are overwhelming! It is in troubles like this that we must trust in the mercy and grace of God with all our heart. He cares. He loves us unconditionally.

When we choose to wait on God in times like these, God binds us together with all that He is, exchanging our weakness for His strength. And then, we mount up with wings of eagles, run and don't get tired, and wait and do not get weary. What an awesome and loving God we serve!

My Reflections   *Date*_____

40

Fear of "Hello"

Delight yourself in the Lord; and He will give you the desires of your heart. Commit your way to the Lord, trust also in Him, and He will do it (Psalm 37:4-5).

I do not have an outgoing personality, so meeting people has always been a challenge for me. It is so much easier for me to speak to a group than it is to talk one-on-one. What do you say after "My name is ..." and "How are you?"

I know that I am not alone in this and that there are many more like me who are called to proclaim God's Word, minister His grace and mercy, and reveal His love. But what holds us back is this one lie that the enemy uses to hinder us: "I've got nothing to say." It is fear!

But God has not given us a spirit of fear! He has given us a spirit of love, power, and a sound, disciplined mind!

Stepping out is one of the hurdles we must overcome for the sake of the Gospel of our Lord Jesus and for the sake of all the hurting people who have been forced into the enemy's awful afflictions. God has placed hurting people in our path so that we can share His truth with them. It all begins with an introduction of who we are, and that is hard to do if we don't move past the lie of the enemy that would holds us back!

Jesus is about people. If we commit our way to the Lord and trust Him, the words we need will be there. Faith begins with the first step.

My Reflections   *Date*_____

41

Step on Stepping Stones

Therefor there is now no condemnation for those who are in Christ Jesus (Romans 8:1).

There is no condemnation for those in Christ Jesus because His life is in us through His Holy Spirit. He sets us free of condemnation if we have missed the mark called *sin,* and then have truly repented and keep going forward. We need to know this because many people are stopped in their tracks, unable to fulfill the call of God because of condemnation and feelings of unworthiness.

God did not create us to wallow in condemnation, but instead to be saturated with His presence and love. Yes, what we have done may carry a penalty, but through heartfelt repentance we can receive God's forgiveness and move forward in Christ.

Too many Christians feel like blobs under a blood covering because of what they call their *failures.* But those failures can create stepping stones. *Repentance* is a stepping stone! *Accepting our forgiveness* from God is a stepping stone. *Stepping out of condemnation* is a stepping stone. *God's Word* is a stepping stone. All of these stepping stones lead to freedom in Christ Jesus and help get us back on track so we can fulfill God's plan and purpose for our life. Step on the stepping stones! Keep moving forward!

My Reflections   *Date*_____

42

God Takes Care of the Lilies

"And why are you anxious about clothing? Observe how the lilies of the field grow; they do not toil nor do they spin" (Matthew 6:28).

Jesus asks, "Why are you anxious about clothing?"

In our world, the thoughts about clothing might be, "How can I purchase this outfit, or the material needed to make this outfit?" But in Biblical times, making a garment consumed a lot of time and energy. First, linen or wool would have to be woven into thread and then made into cloth. It was a time-consuming process.

Today people are consumed with the needs of daily life and physical things, and there is a tendency to forget what is most important. What is important is time spent seeking the Kingdom of God and His righteousness, learning His Word and His ways. God promises to take care of our needs and to bless us so that we can be a blessing to others. God takes care of the lilies. God will take care of you and me.

My Reflections   *Date*_____

43

God Rebuilds Ruins

Beloved, I pray that in all respects you may prosper and be in good health, just as your soul prospers (3 John 1:2).

God Word is truth and it does not change. God cannot change. Circumstances do, but God does not. He is good, and He is the God who brings increase and blessing.

Third John 1:2 says that this is what God wants for us as we renew our minds—as we bring our thoughts into agreement with His Word. And as we deposit His Word in our hearts, that Word will produce faith.

Often things come at us that we know are not of God. They are not His desire for our life, and they are not the abundant life that Jesus came to give us. Then shame tries to come in and create in us a sense of failure. Shame will try to convince us that we are a bad witness and that we are merely tolerated or treated with mercy because we have accepted Jesus as our Lord! But the truth is that we are not qualified to receive God's blessings based on our own performance or on anything the enemy can get us to believe.

Jesus came to set us free from all the lies of the enemy, to dress us in His joy, and to plant us solidly in righteousness, as solid as an oak tree. God will take what has been ruined in our lives and rebuild it. He will bring health and prosperity to us. We will be called the ministers of God, and instead of the shame the enemy tried to give us, we will be given a double portion of God's joy.

We must not put our trust in other people; our trust must be only in our Lord Jesus Christ! We can trust that we are loved by Almighty God. We can trust the Holy Spirit to lead and guide us. If we will keep our focus on God only, and trust Him, not looking to people or circumstances, we will increase. How can we not flourish when we are getting to know God and His Word more and more?

My Reflections   *Date*_____

❧❧ 44 ❧❧

Step into It

"The LORD makes poor and rich;
He brings low, He also exalts.
⁸"He raises the poor from the dust,
He lifts the needy from the ash heap
To make them sit with nobles,
And inherit a seat of honor;
For the pillars of the earth are the LORD'S,
And He set the world on them.
⁹"He keeps the feet of His godly ones,
But the wicked ones are silenced in darkness;
For not by might shall a man prevail.
"Those who contend with the LORD will be shattered;
Against them He will thunder in the heavens,
The LORD will judge the ends of the earth;
And He will give strength to His king,
And will exalt the horn of His anointed"
(1 Samuel 2:7-10).

Sometimes as we walk through this life, we begin to take inventory of where we have been, where we are now, and where we are going. Then we ask ourselves if we have walked the path that God has chosen for us. Even if we are doing and saying all the right things, we'll never be as successful or as prosperous as we would be if we were on the path God has called us to walk.

There are times the path we are walking on seems to

change. Even if our direction seems unsure, we can count on God to keep us on His path, going in His direction. We can count on God to increase our peace and joy because we have the confidence we are doing exactly what He wants for this season in our lives.

Even then, we must also be open to allow God to promote us into other areas that we may know nothing about. God is going to bring many of us out of our comfort zones and into places we never dreamed of or thought possible. God will bring a flow of finances to accomplish His purpose and many people who are in this season of life will begin to find God's purpose stirring on the inside. Step into it!

My Reflections   *Date*_____

45

We Are in Good Hands

> The Lord is my shepherd, I shall not want. He makes me lie down in green pastures; He leads me beside quiet waters. He restores my soul; He guides me in the paths of righteousness For His name's sake (Psalm 23:1-3).

As we think about the greatness of our God and how He sets things in motion in our lives, it is so amazing to realize how much He loves us and continues to set us on the path He has chosen. And to help us, He sent Jesus and the Holy Spirit.

When children are walking with their mom or dad and something catches their attention, more than likely, they will step off the path. But the voice or the gentle hand of their loving parent nudges them back onto the right path, keeping them safe and pointed in the right direction. It is important because that path is the only path that will take them to the right destination.

The Bible tells us that the Lord will never leave us nor forsake us. It also tells us that He is the same yesterday, today, and tomorrow. It tells us He has a plan for our lives, a plan that gives us a future and a hope. We are not to not lean on our own understanding, but on Him, and He will direct our path. Sounds to me like we are in good hands!

My Reflections   *Date*_____

46

Stop the Pit Bulls. Be Territorial.

Behold, I have given you authority to tread upon serpents and scorpions, and over all the power of the enemy, and nothing shall injure you (Luke 10:19).

One day, I was sitting outdoors enjoying the weather and letting my baby dog do his thing. Our yard was separated from our next-door neighbor's yard by a six-foot, wooden fence. Our neighbor's pit bull had always been friendly—until now! Suddenly, that dog grew vicious, and with teeth showing, he tried to come over the fence and attack my little dog.

Such an attack in our own backyard can catch us off guard because it is where we feel safe. It is not the place we would expect to be attacked.

Sometimes the same kind of attack can hit us unexpectedly on a personal level. It comes through people who have always seemed so friendly, but suddenly they make life difficult for us. They do or say things that create fear and distrust, and that might even bring destruction.

We live in such a competitive world! We see it in society's addiction to sports. It shows up in our dog-eat-dog world. But we don't have to fall into this way of life and succumb to the ways of this world because we are citizens of a different world—a heavenly kingdom.

Romans 5:5 tells us that we have the love of God dwelling in us. It is a part of our nature. So, remembering this, how do we deal with the attacks of the enemy? We know that these attacks have a spiritual root, that people are not the enemy.

We can overcome! We walk in the authority given to us through the Name of Jesus and the Word of God, authority that is available because of the redeeming Blood of Jesus.

We use the common sense that God has put within us, letting the Holy Spirit guide us to put up protecting walls against the attacks. We build fences by using the Word.

Psalms 91 is a psalm of protection from the enemy's attacks. Verses 14-16 remind us that, because of our love and trust in our Heavenly Lord, He has promised to deliver us from destruction. That includes the sudden attack that would have viciously killed my little dog and crushed my heart. In the same way, God wants to protect us from the pit bulls of life. He wants to keep them out of our backyard. He wants us to live in His peace and under His protection.

If the enemy tries to jump our fence, we are to take our authority in God's Word to keep him out. Be territorial!

My Reflections   *Date*_____

۞۞ 47 ۞۞

Possess Your Land

Now Elisha spoke to the woman whose son he had restored to life, saying, "Arise and go with your household, and sojourn wherever you can sojourn; for the Lord has called for a famine, and it shall even come on the land for seven years." So the woman arose and did according to the word of the man of God, and she went with her household and sojourned in the land of the Philistines seven years. And it came about at the end of seven years the woman returned from the land of the Philistines; and she went out to appeal to the king for her house and for her field ... . When the king asked the woman, she related it to him. So the king appointed for her a certain officer, saying, "Restore all that was hers and all the produce of the field from the day that she left the land even until now" (2 Kings 8:1-3, 6).

People can be living in a place that is not the best. They are in a place called *survival* after a serious situation and are getting by the best they can.

In this passage, Elisha told the woman to go back to where she belonged, to return to her homeland. After returning, as he had directed, she approached the king to re-establish ownership of her home and her land (Note: It was *her* land). The king's responded in her favor, restoring to her the property that was rightfully hers. He even appointed a supervisor to ensure that no one would stop her from possessing what was hers!

God, Our King, is calling for people to come back to our dwelling place in Christ Jesus and to possess what He has provided for us. God will restore to us the things that have been stolen from us. Many of us have felt as if we have been living in a wilderness, and in fact, we have been! But God is drawing us out of the wilderness and into the place of provision.

Let me encourage you to be like the woman in II Kings and don't allow fear to keep you from asking for what is rightfully yours. Go in faith! Let God restore. This is our day to possess our home and land in God's Kingdom.

My Reflections   *Date*_____

৺৺ 48 ৺৺

Why Is This Happening?

Then Gideon said to him, "O my lord, if the Lord is with us, why then has all this happened to us? And where are all His miracles which our fathers told us about, saying, 'Did not the Lord bring us up from Egypt?' But now the Lord has abandoned us and given us into the hand of Midian" (Judges 6:13).

Gideon and his family were in a terrible situation. The pit where he was beating out wheat for survival was, in fact, keeping him hidden from the enemy. This particular pit had been created as a place to make wine, a symbol of joy, but situations in life had stolen Gideon's joy. He was just existing. He was in *the hole of barely getting by*.

Gideon's was hiding from the Midianites, a very evil people. They would attack and rob the Israelites. In the process, what they couldn't plunder, they would destroy. It was not an easy time for Gideon and the rest of God's people, yet God was working on a plan for them.

God's heart is for His people. He can cause a nobody like Gideon—filled with fear of the enemy and hiding in a pit—to rise up and use a small, untrained army to overpower the tactics of the enemy.

"Why is this happening?" Gideon asks.

"Well now, Gideon, maybe it is because you are not doing anything to stop it!"

"But I am only one person!" Gideon's might respond.

"Gideon, one person who will obey God can turn a nation of pitiful people into victors. Gideon, you must decide to get out of the hole. Stand up! Destroy your false idols! Be a doer of God's Word! Trust in God and walk in the Holy Spirit's powerful anointing. Gideon, it is your choice to stay in the hole or to arise to fulfill God's ordained plan for you."

God has called each one of us—male and female, rich and poor, young and old, regardless of social status—to rise up and get out of the pit and make a difference. The first step of faith out of the pit may not be easy, but with God you are more than a conqueror.

Be encouraged. God is for you and not against you. God's heart always wants the best for you. You are special to Him! Arise and shine for God's glory.

My Reflections   *Date*_____

❦❦ 49 ❦❦

Whose Report?

She went and reported to those who had been with Him, while they were mourning and weeping. When they heard that He was alive and had been seen by her, they refused to believe it.... Afterward He appeared to the eleven themselves as they were reclining at the table; and He reproached them for their unbelief and hardness of heart, because they had not believed those who had seen Him after He had risen. (Mark 16:10-11, 16).

Whose report will you believe? Will you believe the Word of the Lord, spoken through an anointed person? Or would you rather believe the reporting of the news or the reports of unbelievers?

The Disciples were rebuked because they did not believe, and perhaps, for having hardness of heart toward Mary—a woman—the one sent with the good news that Jesus had risen from the dead.

The choice is yours. Will you believe the naysayers? Or will you believe those who speak the truth of God's Word? Whose report will you believe?

I will believe the report of the Lord!

My Reflections   *Date*_____

ೊಳಿ 50 ೊಳಿ

Come!

But seeing the wind, he became afraid, and beginning to sink, he cried out, saying, "Lord, save me!" And immediately Jesus stretched out His hand and took hold of him, and said to him, "O you of little faith, why did you doubt?" (Matthew 14:30-31).

In Matthew 14, the Disciples were in a powerful, life-threatening storm in the middle of the Sea of Galilee. Suddenly, they saw Jesus approaching them, walking on the water. It seemed to them that it must be a ghost! But Peter decided he was going to find out if this really was Jesus. So, he asked Jesus to tell him to come. Jesus said, "Come."

Immediately, Peter got out of the boat and walked toward Jesus. He was walking on the water!

Had he stayed in the boat he might have died. So, whether in the boat or on the sea, it was *sink or swim!* This storm made it impossible to swim!

When Jesus said "Come," Peter heard the Lord's spoken command, and immediately, he acted on it. He jumped in with both feet.

Sometimes in the storms of life—even though it doesn't make sense to our natural thinking—we need to jump in with both feet. We need to move out of the comfort zone of the boat. It will stretch our faith, but we need to do it!

Yes, like Peter, we may begin to sink, but Jesus won't let us drown. He will challenge us to develop our faith.

The choice for us, as believers, is this: Stay in the boat and drown, or jump in with both feet and let Jesus lead to a place of peace and safety.

I believe I hear Jesus saying, "Come!"

My Reflections   *Date*_____

❧❧ 51 ❧❧

Stir Up the Gifts

> For this reason I remind you to kindle afresh the gift of God which is in you through the laying on of my hands. For God has not given us a spirit of timidity, but of power and love and discipline. Therefore do not be ashamed of the testimony of our Lord or of me His prisoner, but join with me in suffering for the gospel according to the power of God, who has saved us and called us with a holy calling, not according to our works, but according to His own purpose and grace which was granted us in Christ Jesus from all eternity, but now has been revealed by the appearing of our Savior Christ Jesus, who abolished death and brought life and immortality to light through the gospel, for which I was appointed a preacher and an apostle and a teacher (2 Timothy 1:6-11).

We need to be reminded to stir up the gifts that God has placed within us. We do that by meditating on His Word, and then, by stepping forth to do as the Holy Spirit leads.

The first thing we must do, however, is to recognize God's gifts and calling. That is not pride, but an acceptance of the responsibility that goes with obedience to God's plan and purpose for our lives.

So often we allow those things God wants to promote and bring forth through us to be pressed down and quenched by the voice of others, by the traditions of religion, and by the bondage of fear. So often we have allowed others—and even ourselves—to limit our lives. We confine ourselves to a well-defined box. We climb in mentally and close the lid! We may become somewhat comfortable and even content. But that is not God's heart for us.

It is time to step out of the box, stir ourselves up, and fulfill God's plan and purpose for our lives. If we are unsure how to do this, we can ask Him to show us and then we can start walking. God will guide us.

My Reflections   *Date*_____

52

Strength in Weariness

> Do you not know? Have you not heard? The Everlasting God, the Lord, the Creator of the ends of the earth does not become weary or tired. His understanding is inscrutable. He gives strength to the weary. And to him who lacks might He increases power. Though youths grow weary and tired, And vigorous young men stumble badly, Yet those who wait for the Lord will gain new strength; They will mount up with wings like eagles, They will run and not get tired, They will walk and not become weary (Isaiah 40:28-31).

I have had the opportunities to overcome weariness. But in the midst of times like that, I have remembered that God has promised to give strength to those who wait on Him. We *wait on Him* by giving attention to and receiving His promise.

The word *wait* means "to bind together and to tarry in expectancy." So, when we wait on the Lord, we are bound together with Him in expectancy. In other words, we can confidently expect to receive strength in exchange for weariness. Since God never wearies, the exchange of strength for weariness is powerful!!

Off to work now, in the power and strength of the Lord!

My Reflections   *Date*_____

❧❧ 53 ❧❧

Faith Is the Believer's Way of Life

> The apostles said to the Lord, "Increase our faith!" And the Lord said, "If you had faith like a mustard seed, you would say to this mulberry tree, 'Be uprooted and be planted in the sea'; and it would obey you. "Which of you, having a slave plowing or tending sheep, will say to him when he has come in from the field, 'Come immediately and sit down to eat'? "But will he not say to him, 'Prepare something for me to eat, and properly clothe yourself and serve me while I eat and drink; and afterward you may eat and drink'? "He does not thank the slave because he did the things which were commanded, does he? "So you too, when you do all the things which are commanded you, say, 'We are unworthy slaves; we have done only that which we ought to have done'" (Luke 17:5-10).

As I was reading my Bible this morning, this passage of scripture jumped out at me. I remembered that faith is a natural response with corresponding action in our life. So, as was the case of the servant in this passage, our daily walk releases faith as we go about our daily activities. Serving and being a witness for God, keeping our focus steadfastly doing the things that are pleasing, and being confident that our needs will be met, are all keys to growing in faith.

My Reflections   *Date*_____

❧❧ 54 ❧❧

Jesus Is the Answer

> And Jesus stopped and said, "Call him here." So they called the blind man, saying to him, "Take courage, stand up! He is calling for you." Throwing aside his cloak, he jumped up and came to Jesus. And answering him, Jesus said, "What do you want Me to do for you?" And the blind man said to Him, "Rabboni, I want to regain my sight!" And Jesus said to him, "Go; your faith has made you well." Immediately he regained his sight and began following Him on the road (Mark 10:49-52).

Blind Bartimaeus was a loser. He was someone to throw a coin at if you felt like it. Or maybe he was just someone to ignore. He would be dusty and dirty from sitting alongside of the road. Maybe kids threw rocks at him! Maybe others lowered themselves to calling him ugly names. Whatever the case, there was no way out for him. BUT JESUS! The people tried to shut him up, but his heart said, "No way!"

Jesus hears us no matter where we are in life. He came to remove the blinders from our eyes! He came to set us free from the darkness that surrounds us.

Jesus gave Bartimaeus three things that He wants all of us to have.

1. Jesus gave him *recognition.* Even though the crowd

had discounted him, but Jesus did not. Jesus acknowledged him.

2. Jesus gave him *sight* to see as he had never seen before, or at least, not for a long time.
3. Jesus gave him *purpose,* a reason for living.

Bartimaeus had more insight than did the people around him who could see. He called Jesus, *the Son of David,* which is a messianic title. No matter where you are or where you have been, Jesus is always the answer!

My Reflections   *Date*_____

✽✽ 55 ✽✽

The Cell Phone

Let your character be free from the love of money, being content with what you have; for He Himself has said, "I will never desert you, nor will I ever forsake you" (Hebrews 13:5).

The cell phone is a wonderful piece of technology, especially when we need it. With it, I can communicate with others and I can get information and direction. But this is true only if it is with me wherever I go.

This tremendous little piece of technology must have its power charged up to be ready for use.

Do I need my cell phone 24 hours a day, seven days a week? No. I need it when communication is required! But even then, the cell phone must be where I am.

Jesus said that He would never leave or forsake us. But how many times do we leave Him at home? How often do we not pay attention to His communication to us throughout the day? The Holy Spirit indwells us to lead, guide, comfort, and direct us, speaking to us what God is saying.

On a certain day, I thought my cell phone was in my purse, but it wasn't. I had accidently left it at home. This meant that I had no phone communication with others. But thankfully, this is never the case with the

Lord. I am never without The One Who communicates with me all the time, wherever I am and whenever it is needed—which is 24 hours a day, seven days a week. The only *device* I need is my listening receivers!

My Reflections *Date*_____

☙ 56 ☙

God Has a Good Plan

Thou wilt make known to me the path of life; In Thy presence is fulness of joy; In Thy right hand there are pleasures forever (Psalm 16:11).

In our daily walk we are confronted with so many choices and we have to make so many decisions. Our minds can become overwhelmed. We can try to manage our thoughts, but we find our directions questioned and our plans disrupted. But if we will let God put His thoughts in our heart, then the plan He gives us will bring His peace. In that peace we find fullness of joy, and as we follow God's directions, we also find success.

This morning, as I was listening to God, I believe He showed me that He had thwarted many attacks against me and my family. I am so grateful for His goodness and protection. I am thankful that He loves me unconditionally and that He is so involved in my life. What a joy to have the privilege and honor of walking in His ways, bringing glory and honor to the Name of Jesus. God has a good plan for all of us. It is a plan for victory!

My Reflections   *Date*_____

∾ 57 ∾

Joy Testimony

The thief comes only in order to steal and kill and destroy. I came that they may have and enjoy life, and have it in abundance [to the full, till it overflows] (John 10:10, Amplified).

Those cell phones! Last night my cell phone was not working properly, but this morning it is working just fine. Since I didn't know that it wasn't working, I missed a call that was a very special moment in our lives. The enemy robbed us!

At 11:30 that same evening, we received a call on our house phone. What an awesome call it was! Someone we greatly love was calling to tell about experiencing the presence of the Lord, and about being on fire for Him! What joy! What excitement!

It seems that this person's phone had accidently called us, and when we tried to return her call, she didn't answer. When she saw that we had called, she knew she had to share what God had done, and we finally heard from her what God had done in her life. God is faithful! What an awesome God we serve. Even though I am tired this morning, I am walking on air!

My Reflections   *Date*_____

~ 58 ~

God Is There

The Spirit of the Lord God is upon me, because the Lord has anointed me to bring good news to the afflicted; He has sent me to bind up the brokenhearted, to proclaim liberty to captives, and freedom to prisoners; to proclaim the favorable year of the Lord, and the day of vengeance of our God; to comfort all who mourn, to grant those who mourn in Zion, giving them a garland instead of ashes, the oil of gladness instead of mourning, the mantle of praise instead of a spirit of fainting. So they will be called oaks of righteousness, the planting of the Lord, that He may be glorified (Isaiah 61:1-3).

Isaiah 61 is so full of promise! It is a scripture that brings comfort, strength, and restoration. It shows us a future full of the love and the goodness of God. We can trust and rejoice continuously in God, despite what the enemy and the world is throwing at us.

My Iowa relatives, along with thousands of others, lived for weeks under the threat of their homes and jobs being washed away by the flooding Missouri River. As if this were not enough, tornadoes were threatening to add to the devastation. In the midst of it all, God brought peace to my heart, helping me to know that all would be well. While speaking Psalm 91 over them, I knew God's Word would not return to Him void, but would accomplish all it is sent to do.

As we go through the storms and trials that life throws at us, we can rest in peace, trusting fully in God. It may be harder for those who are not in the situation, since it means watching and standing helplessly by, while not being able to do anything.

But we are able to do something! We can pray, praise, and worship God. We can trust Him for deliverance and healing, whereas those in the situation may be so overwhelmed that they can't. This is how we can come aside and lift the arms that hang down in weariness—not from a lack of trust in God—but from the emotional fatigue, ongoing physical demands, and the long duration of the difficult circumstances. This is called *The Love of Family*. And all of this is ours because we are part of The Family of God.

My Reflections   *Date*_____

☙ 59 ❧

See the Tree, Not the Forest

And He said to them, "Go into all the world and preach the gospel to all creation" (Mark 16:15).

Believers are called to share The Good News. Many times, however—to use a picture to illustrate—we can't see the trees because of the forest all around us.

In the midst of it all, we must remember that God's promises never fail. His Word is true.

Yesterday was one of those times when the little foxes were trying to spoil the vine, but praise sent them running every time they attacked.

First, I locked my keys in the house, but I was able to get in to retrieve them.

Then, my computer at the office decided not to work properly, but I was able to get it back up and running. Praise the Lord!

Next, someone gave me a bad report and I realized it was a lie the enemy wanted me to accept. Won't do it! Praise the Lord!

Then, my son took a bad fall and he landed in a way that could have broken his arm—but it didn't break!

Praise the Lord!

By mistake, I left my phone in a public restroom, only to have some kind soul put it in a safe place until I got it back. Praise the Lord!

I could go on and on, using yesterday as an example of the continued goodness of God that was so evident in each situation.

But maybe, now, it's time for you to take a moment to look at the goodness of God in your life. By taking your eyes off *the forest,* you will be able to see God at work on your behalf. God wants you to see His goodness because He loves you so much!

My Reflections　　　　*Date*_____

❧❧ 60 ❧❧

Judge Them Loved

Now on the same occasion there were some present who reported to Him about the Galileans, whose blood Pilate had mingled with their sacrifices. And He answered and said to them, "Do you suppose that these Galileans were greater sinners than all other Galileans, because they suffered this fate? "I tell you, no, but unless you repent, you will all likewise perish. "Or do you suppose that those eighteen on whom the tower in Siloam fell and killed them, were worse culprits than all the men who live in Jerusalem? "I tell you, no, but unless you repent, you will all likewise perish" (Luke 13:1-5).

My heart goes out to my neighbors to the south of us. They suffered through terrible fires, and now it's floods. Having gone through several disasters myself, I know how devastating it is, not just physically, but emotionally, as well. I know the questions one asks.

When we see this kind of devastation, some people will say it is God's wrath poured out in judgment because of rampant sin in the area. But God is not the author of destruction, nor does He use it to teach us a lesson, as many would say!

The fact is that we live in a fallen world where bad things happen that should not happen. We see this in the scripture, specifically in Luke 13:1-5. It describes a situation in which bad things had happened to people. When Jesus was asked about the situation, He replied that those people were not worse sinners than anyone else, so instead of judging them and the situation, they should take a look at their own lives.

Where do you stand?

If you were the one going through a difficult situation, where would your faith be? Good question!

If we are going to stand in judgment, let us judge these people as loved by God and pray for them.

My Reflections *Date*_____

≈≈ 61 ≈≈

God Gives Grace and Favor

The steps of a man are established by the Lord; and He delights in his way (Psalm 37:23).

Well, I did it again. I overslept. My alarm kept yelling at me, and I kept hitting it and telling it to shut up.

I wonder how many times we do that to the Holy Spirit when He is trying to get us to arise and get going.

"Just five more minutes of sleep and I will get going." We hit the alarm again and moan, "Just another five minutes."

Suddenly, we realize it's too late to do everything we needed to do to start the day off right. But thank God! We can cry out for His grace and favor. And thank God! The Holy Spirit will continue to lead and guide us throughout the day, despite our shortcomings.

Thank God, too, that even my little dog will forgive me when I get home tonight after I didn't have the time to cuddle and play with him before going to work!!

God is good.

Now, where is the tape to tack up that hem that just came undone?

My Reflections   *Date*_____

❧❧ 62 ❧❧

Faith Is for Children

Then some children were brought to Him so that He might lay His hands on them and pray; and the disciples rebuked them. But Jesus said, "Let the children alone, and do not hinder them from coming to Me; for the kingdom of heaven belongs to such as these" (Matthew 19:13-14).

Faith is not only an *adult* thing. Faith is the way that we must walk as believers. And it is with child-like faith that we please God. This is important because *without faith it is impossible to please God.*

With that thought in mind let me ask a few questions.

- Do you believe any of these children who came to Jesus felt that He didn't love them or that He didn't care about them?

- Do you believe that any of these children tried to do works to get blessed by Him?

- Do you believe that the children were aware of their social status, their gender, or their nationality when they came near Jesus?

- Do you believe that the children were excited to be in His presence?

- Do you think that the children cared that there were some religious bullies or some well-meaning people that didn't like the idea of the children being there? Hmmmm?

As adults, let's come to Jesus with the heart of a child—in trust, in faith, and with expectation!

My Reflections   *Date*_____

⚜ 63 ⚜

Trees

"Blessed is the man who trusts in the Lord
And whose trust is the Lord.
"For he will be like a tree planted by the water,
That extends its roots by a stream
And will not fear when the heat comes;
But its leaves will be green,
And it will not be anxious in a year of drought
Nor cease to yield fruit (Jeremiah 17:7-8).

Blessed is the man or woman who knows they can trust the Lord God with all their heart.

When we lived in the Las Vegas area, I noticed that some trees managed to survive in the desert, even in the sandy desert around Lake Mead. Despite the harsh conditions, they put down roots and survived the heat.

We also lived in Wyoming, and in Buford, along I-80, a tree is growing out of a huge boulder. In fact, it is a famous landmark called *The Tree in the Rock.*

Where streams and rivers flow through rich farm land, trees flourish along the banks, abundantly supplied with water.

Then, there are trees that have been transplanted from their natural habitat, such as the palm trees in Las Vegas.

We usually don't think about all that these trees have overcome to exist. In the same way, we see people where they are "planted," but we don't see what they have had to overcome to flourish or even to survive.

But God sees. God cares. It is the Lord God Almighty Who gives us the strength to stand, the hope to press on, and the ability to grow. Our part is to trust Him completely and to rely on His ability. Only then can we be all that we were created to be.

As a woman minister, called by God to teach and minister His Word, I have struggled against serious opposition, including such things as public ridicule. Yet, it is challenges like this that actually cause us to grow stronger in the Lord. It is this opposition to our heavenly calling that causes us to be able to be flexible and bend through God's abundant grace. That grace keeps us from becoming brittle and bitter. Through it all, God strengthens us in His *agape* love. Knowing that we can trust God and that He lives big in us enables us to continue to produce fruit that brings life to others as they receive from us.

I may not be as beautiful as an old oak tree, but I am the tree God created me to be. I am planted by the water of God's Holy Word growing and I am still producing!

My Reflections   *Date*_____

64

Bad Attitude Day

This is the message we have heard from Him and announce to you, that God is Light, and in Him there is no darkness at all. If we say that we have fellowship with Him and yet walk in the darkness, we lie and do not practice the truth; but if we walk in the Light as He Himself is in the Light, we have fellowship with one another, and the blood of Jesus His Son cleanses us from all sin. If we say that we have no sin, we are deceiving ourselves and the truth is not in us. If we confess our sins, He is faithful and righteous to forgive us our sins and to cleanse us from all unrighteousness (1 John 1:5-9).

Therefore there is now no condemnation for those who are in Christ Jesus. For the law of the Spirit of life in Christ Jesus has set you free from the law of sin and of death (Romans 8:1-2).

Yesterday started with the alarm ringing at five a.m. and ended with my head hitting the pillow after 10:30 p.m. From start to finish, it had been one of those days when *little foxes were trying to spoil the vine (See Song of Solomon 2:15).*

How? The hot water refused to shut off when I drew my morning bath. Then, my computers quit, putting me behind in my work. I finally caught a quick supper at bedtime. It had been a long, hard day!

Well, I had failed the test, and my attitude needed a major overhaul. Things that normally would have run off my back—like the proverbial water on a duck's back—were not running off my back!

When these *little foxes* came along to steal my peace, I allowed my flesh to rule and to determine my responses. (In other words, I failed the test!) But Jesus is quick to forgive. He restores us, and I am grateful!

When I find myself in this situation, here's what I do.

- I *recognize* I am walking in darkness and need the light of God's Word to shine on my heart.
- I *repent* by doing a 180 degree turn and totally going the other direction.
- I *confess* I know it is my fault and I don't put blame on anyone else, even when other people are involved. After all, *people are people*. They are called human beings because that is what they are being.
- I *receive forgiveness* from the Lord.
- I finish by **giving God praises and thanksgiving.**

Now, I am sure most of you never have days like this! But if you come across someone who is having a bad day, it will be your opportunity to help them get the little foxes out of the garden of their heart.

May you have a wonderful, blessed day, and may you experience God's love, joy, and peace.

My Reflections   *Date*_____

∾ 65 ∾

God Is Today

For God so loved the world, that He gave His only begotten Son, that whoever believes in Him shall not perish, but have eternal life (John 3:16).

This is a familiar scripture, often memorized and quoted. If you ask someone what this scripture is about, they will probably say that it is about God and being *born again* because Jesus died for us. That's right! But there is so much more. It says *whoever* believes in Him shall not perish. Are you a *whoever*? Perish from what? And how?

This promise is given to those who choose to walk in faith. It means that we will not be destroyed. We will have eternal life. God is the I AM, not the God of yesterday, or tomorrow, or someday. God is always now, and He has given to us *zoe* life; that is, the *God - kind of life*.

But unless we know it, we cannot walk in it. We will keep looking to *a someday*, instead of receiving it *today. Give us this day our daily bread (Mt. 6:11).* **This day!** God is now!

We are to have faith, but not for ourselves alone. Faith enables us to go beyond our own needs and to be a blessing to others. God Himself went beyond His desire for fellowship with us to give us eternal life.

We, too, should go beyond our self-centered needs and let the benefits and reality of eternal life flow to others today!

My Reflections   *Date*_____

❦❦ 66 ❦❦

Focused, Not Fearful

> Search me, O God, and know my heart; try me and know my anxious thoughts; and see if there be any hurtful way in me, and lead me in the everlasting way (Psalm 139:23-24).

When I am involved in doing something and someone walks up to me, catching me off guard, I jump. Someone might ask, "What are you afraid of?" Am I afraid? No, I am just focused.

God knows my heart better than I do. He is aware of my attitudes, and He understands my reactions and why I respond in the manner that I do.

In the same way, we can be focused and not afraid when God approaches us. I am so aware that we need God's help in this area, and I know that we will benefit greatly if we will allow Him to show us anything that He would like to change in us—all the way from our heart to our head. And when God does show us something, it is important that we make the changes. We can be focused and not fearful.

My Reflections   *Date* _____

❧❧ 67 ❧❧

The Blame Game

The man said, "The woman whom You gave to be with me, she gave me from the tree, and I ate" (Genesis 3:12).

A person in my life is resistant when I suggest an area that needs changing. You probably have someone like this in your life!

What they are doing isn't working, but rather than accept the fact and take responsibility for the situation, they shift the blame to others.

That is exactly what Adam did in the Garden. He passed the buck, so to speak, and it didn't help him.

When God shines His light on our problem, it is for our good. He knows we need to change and He wants to help us. As we respond to Him, we will be changed from the inside out, becoming more and more what He created us to be. It is worth the process! Passing the buck only leads to failure.

Are we willing to let Him help us where He knows we need to change? Passing the buck—blaming someone or something else for our own problems—only leads to failure.

My Reflections   Date_____

68

Don't Burn Out

Come to Me, all who are weary and heavy-laden, and I will give you rest. Take My yoke upon you, and learn from Me, for I am gentle and humble in heart; and you shall find rest for your souls. For My yoke is easy, and My load is light (Matthew 11:28-30).

Now to Him who is able to do exceeding abundantly beyond all that we ask or think, according to the power that works within us to Him be the glory in the church and in Christ Jesus to all generations forever and ever. Amen (Ephesians 3:20).

Our work load can be overwhelming because we are carrying it ourselves instead of walking with Jesus and letting Him carry the load.

One weight that we may be carrying is dealing with change and the stress that it creates. In most cases, change is not easy, even though it might be for our good. The reality is that life brings change, again and again, demanding that we adjust to new and different circumstances. Through it all, it is important that we walk in God's peace that passes all understanding.

Jesus tells us to walk together with Him and that He would make our load light. If we don't, we will *burn out*.

No matter what the load is that we are carrying—whether it be in relation to our job, our family, our health, our ministry, or our business—let's let Jesus have the load. We can and must let His peace fill us. We can and must allow ourselves to find rest in Him. His yoke is easy, and His load is light. Jesus says, "Come."

My Reflections   *Date*_____

✌ 69 ✌

When You Don't Want To

For I am confident of this very thing, that He who began a good work in you will perfect it until the day of Christ Jesus (Philippians 1:6).

Then Jonah prayed to the Lord his God from the stomach of the fish, and he said, "I called out of my distress to the Lord, and He answered me. I cried for help from the depth of Sheol; Thou didst hear my voice" (Jonah 2:1-2).

The account of Jonah and the fish—not a whale, as tradition teaches—is a wonderful story of how God will call someone to come out of their bitterness and unforgiveness to touch the lives of others. In Jonah's case, God was sending him to very evil, heathen people who persecuted and murdered many of Jonah's nation and loved ones.

But Jonah didn't want to spread the message of salvation to these people. His heart just wasn't in it! So, instead of obeying the Lord, he ran away and ended up in the belly of a big fish.

You might say that he had fallen as low as he could go. It was a crisis moment! He would do what God had called him to do or die. One thing he knew for sure: God was his only hope!

But Jonah cried out to the Lord with all his heart. And

God delivered him!

He yielded to God's will. He went to the heathen city of Nineveh where he preached the Word of the Lord to them, and the whole city repented (Jonah 3) and was saved from destruction.

Many of us—maybe most of us—have experienced great heartache because of what others have said or done. Some of us have experienced betrayal, abuse, rape, and rejection. So, when God asks us—as he did Jonah—to go to these people, it is hard. But God wants the lost to hear His Word and be saved, and he wants us to be His instruments of salvation, healing, and deliverance.

He also wants our wounded hearts to be released from bitterness and purged of unforgiveness. God is faithful, and so we can rest in the assurance that He will, in His great love, continue to perfect us.

My Reflections　　　　　　*Date*_____

৵৵ 70 ৵৵

Advancing

Brethren, I do not regard myself as having laid hold of it yet; but one thing I do: forgetting what lies behind and reaching forward to what lies ahead, I press on toward the goal for the prize of the upward call of God in Christ Jesus (Philippians 3:13-14).

Over the years, I have organized conferences, calling them *advances*, not *retreats*. God's people are called to be advancing always. Even when we are resting, we can be advancing.

Some time ago, I started a group called *The Action Company*, based on Psalm 68:11, which reads: *The Lord gives the command; The women who proclaim the good tidings are a great host.* When it was time for me to advance to other adventures, I had to hand the group over to the next person called to lead it. I literally passed the baton.

It is that way when we are advancing in life and in the call of God on our life. We must let go of the old, whether it is good or bad. The past is too heavy to carry forward.

Advancing means "moving forward, one step at a time, from where we are being released to where we are to go." To do this, we must let go of anything from the past that is holding us back.

Advancing means walking through the doors that God has opened for us for such a time as this.

So, let's advance! Let's minister the Word of God and touch lives, all for the Glory of God.

My Reflections   *Date*_____

71

Forget Not God's Benefits

Bless the Lord, O my soul; And all that is within me, bless His holy name. Bless the Lord, O my soul, And forget none of His benefits (Psalm 103:1-2).

The Lord tells us not to forget His benefits. If the Lord tells us not to forget, there is likely the possibility that we can or will forget.

We may know the promises of God, but when we are hit by one of life's storms, do we settle for less than what God's Word promises?

The bad, negative things that we see and feel can make us forget God's promised benefits, but when we hold God's Word in our heart, the Holy Spirit can bring it to our remembrance at just the right moment.

It may not look or feel as if we have the promises,

So will My word be which goes forth from My mouth;
It will not return to Me empty,
Without accomplishing what I desire,
And without succeeding in the matter for which I sent it
(Isaiah 55:11).

God is faithful. Situations are subject to change, but God's Word will not change.

My Reflections *Date*_____

‥ 72 ‥

Touch the Little Ones

The people brought children to Jesus, hoping he might touch them. The disciples shooed them off. But Jesus was irate and let them know it: "Don't push these children away. Don't ever get between them and me. These children are at the very center of life in the kingdom. Mark this: Unless you accept God's kingdom in the simplicity of a child, you'll never get in." Then, gathering the children up in his arms, he laid his hands of blessing on them (Mark 10:13-16, as paraphrased in *The Message*).

Children are a blessing, gifts from the Lord. I am blessed with two children whom I love greatly, as well as with the *in-loves* they added to our family when they married.

As I read this passage, it came to mind how the world is doing everything it can—through drugs, alcohol, abuse, and so on—to take children away from both their parents and the Kingdom of God. And I've seen the heartache of parents when their child gets caught up in these and other ungodly activities.

The Lord spoke to my heart how important it is that we, as adults, reach out to the little ones now. It only takes a moment to give a hug, *a high five*, or a little wave to those who are shy. As we do these little things out of our heart, we are imparting God's love to them. Then, we can pray for them, as the Lord leads.

Let's help parents as much as we can, by being a Godly example to the little children.

As I am writing this, I am noticing that this is not my *typical* writing, but then, what is my *typical* writing? It is whatever God puts on my heart!

We know we are to come to God as children in childlike faith and trust. As God's women and men, we have to reach out to the little ones, helping them to grow in faith and trust in the Lord. So, let me encourage you to give a little one a moment of your time. I believe God will reward you greatly.

My Reflections   *Date*_____

73

God Hears

> Truly, truly, I say to you, he who believes in Me, the works that I do, he will do also; and greater works than these he will do; because I go to the Father. Whatever you ask in My name, that will I do, so that the Father may be glorified in the Son. If you ask Me anything in My name, I will do it (John 14:12-14).

I have this motto:
> If I ask once, it's a request;
> a second time, it is a reminder;
> but a third time, I'm being forced to beg.

It is rare that I will ask a fourth time, because after a third request, I will generally do it myself or it won't get done.

If I must ask a third time, both trust and respect are being lost. You see, trust and respect are earned, not freely given.

Not so with God! He said that when we pray, He will hear and answer the first time. We can trust God. We don't have to beg Him. So, be thankful and pray, knowing that God will hear and answer.

My Reflections _Date_____

∽ 74 ∽

Be Angry and Sin Not

Be angry, and yet do not sin; do not let the sun go down on your anger, and do not give the devil an opportunity (Ephesians 4:26-27).

Be angry and sin not. Another way I could say this is, "Be angry, but don't get out of faith." We can be angry because of the devil's attacks on family members, and yet, we can stay in faith. In the midst of irritating challenges like that, it is important to stay in faith, because without faith it is impossible to please God (Hebrews 11:6).

God is the only one who can change what, to us, seems impossible. Through His word, His power, and His anointing, He brings the needed change. NOTHING is impossible with God at the helm.

My Reflections   *Date*_____

75

Teach Me, Lord

Teach me Your way, O Lord; I will walk in Your truth; Unite my heart to fear Your name (Psalm 86:11).

Unite my heart. What could this odd statement mean?

God doesn't want our hearts to be *divided*. Our heart can be divided when we are confused, distracted, uncertain, and wavering when we try to understand why something is happening, instead of trusting in the Lord in that situation. In other words, our heart can be *at odds with* or *divided* about God when the struggles of life cause us to focus on the *whys* instead of on the promises. This leads us out of faith, causing our heart to be divided toward God.

Asking questions is not wrong! In fact, asking questions is often how we learn. God knows that people need answers, and He wants us to get our answers from Him and from His Word.

On the other hand, the world—if it can offer an answer at all—has only a temporary one that may seem good for the moment. But then, tomorrow comes!

Focus entirely on Jesus—heart and mind. Give God your undivided attention, knowing *He Is The Answer.*

My Reflections   *Date*_____

❦❦ 76 ❦❦

Don't Get Bitten Twice

Trust in the Lord with all your heart
And do not lean on your own understanding.
In all your ways acknowledge Him,
And He will make your paths straight
(Proverbs 3:5-6).

I once heard a story I have never forgotten. It's the story of a person who walks into someone's yard for the first time. In the yard, unknown to the person, is an unfriendly dog, and the person is immediately bitten by the dog.

This would be considered an accident because the person had entered the yard without knowledge of the dog.

Now, as the story continues, the person enters the same yard, but this time, with the knowledge that there is a dog that will bite. The person gets bitten again, but this it is no accident! It is stupidity gone to seed!

Too often, people get themselves into a situation in which they get bitten, and even though they get out of the situation, they turn right around and do it again!

This often happens to people who have been abused in relationships because they do not know how to stay free. There is an answer! Renewing the mind in God's Word is the first key. Then, out of that, learning to trust God and to be led by the Holy Spirit are further keys.

So then, renewing the mind, learning to trust God, and learning to be led by the Holy Spirit will deliver them from the tendency to get bitten again and again.

My Reflections   *Date*_____

≫ 77 ≪

Going with Jesus

Even though I walk through the valley of the shadow of death, I fear no evil, for You are with me; Your rod and Your staff, they comfort me (Psalm 23:4).

The Valley of the Shadow of Death is an actual place, located on a path between two cities in Israel. It is a barren place in the wilderness, where, because of its formation, sunlight cannot penetrate. This makes it a very dangerous place where thieves lie in wait to rob and kill travelers.

There are times when it feels as if this is where we are spiritually! But in faith, we don't camp in this valley. We travel through safely because Jesus goes with us.

My Reflections *Date*_____

❧❧ 78 ❧❧

Rear-View Mirror Vision

Jesus replied and said, "A man was going down from Jerusalem to Jericho, and fell among robbers, and they stripped him and beat him, and went away leaving him half dead. And by chance a priest was going down on that road, and when he saw him, he passed by on the other side. Likewise, a Levite also, when he came to the place and saw him, passed by on the other side. But a Samaritan, who was on a journey, came upon him; and when he saw him, he felt compassion, and came to him and bandaged up his wounds, pouring oil and wine on them; and he put him on his own beast, and brought him to an inn and took care of him. On the next day he took out two denarii and gave them to the innkeeper and said, 'Take care of him; and whatever more you spend, when I return I will repay you.' Which of these three do you think proved to be a neighbor to the man who fell into the robbers' hands?" And he said, "The one who showed mercy toward him." Then Jesus said to him, "Go and do the same." (Luke 10:30-37).

This story can reveal a lot about each of us. We can get so busy in life that we pass right by opportunities to be a blessing to someone in need. One day I was running late for an appointment when I noticed a man outside a car on the street. It seemed odd, but as I got closer, I realized he was steering his car as he pushed it off the road. When I looked in my rear-view mirror, I noticed two pick-ups driven by men. I assumed they would stop and help him, so I kept going. But when I looked back again, I was surprised to see that both drivers had passed him, without offering help. I was concerned, but I had to keep going because I was on a one-way road with no place to turn around.

Once I arrived at my appointment, I had to sit and wait. As I thought about the situation, I realized that I would have had plenty of time to help him get his car to safety. Sadly, I had missed an opportunity to share Jesus with someone and encourage him amid his troubles. It is a lesson learned!

When I look into the rear-view mirror of life, I want to see people I have touched with the love of God!

My Reflections   *Date*_____

৵৵ 79 ৵৵

Serving Jesus

Let a man regard us in this manner, as servants of Christ, and stewards of the mysteries of God (1 Corinthians 4:1).

You and I are called to be servants under the authority of our Lord Jesus Christ, and we are also called to be stewards, ministers, and carriers of the truth of God's Word. Each of us is called!

Too often, because of wrong teaching and religious tradition, God's Word is held captive, locked up inside a person because of a poor self-image. I believe this has been especially true for women and has kept many from freely sharing God's message with others.

Both men and women must come to the place where they so hate the devil's bondage in people's lives that there is no stopping them from sharing the truth of the Gospel and setting others free.

Through Adam, mankind sinned, giving dominion to the devil, but Jesus came to change that. Jesus—sinless and perfect—died to redeem us and to bring all who would receive Him back into right relationship with God. Jesus didn't stay in the grave, but rose again—Victor over sin, hell, and the grave! Jesus loves us, and it is that love that conquered all. It is God's Word, God's truth, and God's will for us to be free and to be complete in Him. In that freedom, we can see ourselves as God's servants and ministers of the Gospel of our Lord Jesus Christ!

My Reflections   *Date* _____

❦❦ 80 ❦❦

God's Wisdom Is in Us

For consider your calling, brethren, that there were not many wise according to the flesh, not many mighty, not many noble; but God has chosen the foolish things of the world to shame the wise, and God has chosen the weak things of the world to shame the things which are strong, and the base things of the world and the despised, God has chosen, the things that are not, that He might nullify the things that are, that no man should boast before God (1 Corinthians 1:26-29).

The Corinthian church was not made up of highly educated people. In fact, much of the city consisted of a retired military people. Perhaps the city had a lot of women and men with humble hearts towards Jesus. These people were committed to Jesus and were dedicated to following His ways. Nevertheless, Paul had to write to them because of their immaturity and lack of understanding. They were not stupid, but their walk did not rightly reflect Christian values, and they needed guidance and correction. So, Paul was able to help them, and his words encourage us today!

In his letter to the Corinthians, Paul says that God will use people like them—and like us—to spread the Gospel of Jesus Christ. Like Paul and our Corinthian brothers and sisters, we will see people healed, set free, delivered, and most importantly, born-again into the Kingdom of God, with the Holy Spirit dwelling within them, and with the promise of eternal life.

We may not be among the most highly educated in this world, but we do have the wisdom of God in us! *Wisdom* is an attribute from the Lord God Almighty, and that is communicated to us through Jesus, The Word of God, and the Holy Spirit.

Let's walk in this wisdom and allow the Holy Spirit to guide us into all truth. We can be confident, knowing that God has equipped each one of us with His wisdom. We must learn to listen in faith to His voice and to speak what He leads us to speak. It is not for ourselves that we do this, but for others who need us to give them the liberating, saving, healing truth of the Gospel. We are who God wants to use to do this!

My Reflections   *Date*_____

≫ 81 ≪

Being Equipped

Now the God of peace, who brought up from the dead the great Shepherd of the sheep through the blood of the eternal covenant, even Jesus our Lord, equip you in every good thing to do His will, working in us that which is pleasing in His sight, through Jesus Christ, to whom be the glory forever and ever. Amen (Hebrews 13:20-21).

In this passage, the author of the book of Hebrews—whom I believe is probably Priscilla—prays for believers to be equipped with every good thing to do God's will, as He works within us. So often we try to do God's will in our own strength and with our own resources, rather than allowing the Holy Spirit to anoint, lead, guide, and develop us through the Word of God. This would justify our being called *Christians*, which means "Christ-like."

Our purpose on this earth is to reveal God's love. We are equipped for this vital task as we allow the Holy Spirit to be active in our lives, as we spend time in the Word, in prayer, in praise and worship, and as we seek God first.

When we experience a lack of power and anointing in our walk of righteousness, it might be a sign that we have become too program-minded or stuck in a rut!

Or it could be a sign that we have been trying to do God's will in our own way instead of His.

Paul tells us that the gifts and callings of God are *without repentance;* in other words, they are *irrevocable, binding, and irreversible* (Romans 11:29). Nevertheless, without the Holy Spirit's power, they lack the effectiveness needed to make a difference.

There are times when we need to separate ourselves from everything around us so that we can hear clearly what the Holy Spirit is wanting us to say or do.

May we personally receive this prayer recorded in Hebrews by an "unknown author." And may we let the Holy Spirit be the Activator, bringing fullness into our life. I am receiving it!

My Reflections　　　　　*Date*_____

೨ು೨ು 82 ೨ು೨ು

Stuck in a Rut

> Then Peter came and said to Him, "Lord, how often shall my brother sin against me and I forgive him? Up to seven times?" Jesus said to him, "I do not say to you, up to seven times, but up to seventy times seven" (Matthew 18:21-22).

Are you stuck in a rut? Often, the past can do that to us!

Our human bodies continue to advance from day to day, yet they are constantly aging, and our world continues to advance, especially technologically. Despite this, some people are stuck emotionally and mentally, having chosen never to advance. For some reason, they choose not to allow themselves to be more productive in loving and blessing others.

Sometimes, unforgiveness is the problem, causing people to hide their talents, giftings, and callings. In life, things happen that are not good, but healing comes as we step out of the rut and live, not as victims, but as victors, giving God the glory. We can choose to forgive, and when we do, we are no longer captive to mental torment and anguish. We experience peace!

Now, just in case there might be misunderstanding about what I am saying, I want to conclude by making it clear that choosing to forgive does not mean going back into a bad situation, and thereby creating the opportunity for another bad event. Instead, choosing to forgive is choosing not to allow our thoughts to dwell on the events of the past, thus allowing them to get a grip on us and control us.

When we choose to forgive, we are clearing the way for the Holy Spirit to guide us. We are putting ourselves in a place where we can advance and lay hold of the promises of God!

My Reflections *Date*_____

Redemption for All

For God so loved the world, that He gave His only begotten Son, that whoever believes in Him should not perish, but have eternal life (John 3:16).

This is such a familiar verse! It is often read at church services and funerals, and it is usually found in witnessing tracts. But perhaps it is so common that some people think, "I have read this before. I know what it says. I understand it."

But pause for a minute and think about this. In this passage, God isn't talking about things like land, sea, or sky. No! He is talking about *people!* All *people!*

Jesus came to redeem any person who will accept His work on the Cross of Calvary—not just a chosen few, but anyone anywhere. And that tells me that in the Kingdom of God there are no second-class citizens.

My Reflections *Date*_____

84

God's Idea

There is neither Jew nor Greek, there is neither slave nor free man, there is neither male nor female; for you are all one in Christ Jesus (Galatians 3:28).

Jesus came to set all people free from every kind of bondage. In His plan, no one should be held back from being all that He created them to be.

God doesn't want anyone to perish in sin, nor does He want anyone to perish because they are held in bondage by others. God does not want a person's growth stunted.

God's heart is for every one of us to be free to become the wonderful person that He had in mind when He created us (See Psalm 139). Christian life and service is not about roles chosen for us by others nor is it about who is the greatest. It is about letting the love of God flow through us by being the man or woman we were created to be—and that is God's choice.

My Reflections   *Date*_____

৵৵ 85 ৵৵

No Teasing

> And as I began to speak, the Holy Spirit fell upon them just as He did upon us at the beginning. And I remembered the word of the Lord, how He used to say, 'John baptized with water, but you will be baptized with the Holy Spirit.' Therefore if God gave to them the same gift as He gave to us also after believing in the Lord Jesus Christ, who was I that I could stand in God's way? (Acts 11:15-17).

My husband and I were invited to enjoy breakfast with some precious friends. Because of another person who ate with us, I had to put up my guard because this person thinks it is his job to put down women, including me. To him, his remarks are harmless fun, when in fact, they are far from that!

The experience reminds me of how many men and women suffer because of the *harmless teasing* spoken by another person. They defend their actions with statements like, "If I didn't tease them, they wouldn't know I love them."

But whatever happened to the simple words, *I love you?*

Personally, I have learned to let the words that put women down just roll off my back, but I couldn't help but think of those who can't do that or who believe the lie spoken to them.

This Scripture encourages me because, even though much remains to be done to spread the Gospel, no one will be able to stop God's plan, gifts, and callings. This fact holds true for both men and women.

Tradition has put people in categories, and it is hard—but not impossible—for people to think outside these categories. The Holy Spirit is greater than tradition, and He is tearing down the wall of division.

Through God's anointing, the truth of the Gospel will open the eyes of our understanding, helping people see the truth. Jesus went to the Cross, died, and rose again so that all people could be free to walk in unity side-by-side. There are no second-class citizens in the Kingdom of God.

My Reflections   *Date* _____

✨ 86 ✨

Walk in the Promised Land

You divided the sea before them, so that they went through its midst on dry land; their persecutors You threw into the depths, as a stone into mighty waters. Moreover, by a pillar of cloud You led them by day, and by a pillar of fire by night to light the way they should go (Nehemiah 9:11-12, Amplified).

God made a way where there was no way!

Sometimes, as we are serving Jesus, it may seem as if things are coming at us and there is no way out. But just as God made a way for the Israelites, He will make a way for us that will include victory for us and destruction for the enemy.

I was thinking about the healing revivals in Church history. There was opposition. Some people set themselves against the truth of healing found in God's Word, yet God healed.

Human tradition can try to hinder the flow of truth, in the same way that the enemy tries to destroy the release of God's promises. But God is greater, and as we persist in God's truth—standing and believing—we will walk into The Promised Land. God will make the way where there is no way. God will continue—through The Word and by His Holy Spirit—to lead us by day and guide by night.

As God's children—His sons and daughters—and as ministers of the Gospel of Jesus Christ, we can count on His faithfulness to lead us to victory as we pursue His truth and the promises in His Word. We can cross over safely to the other side, as the Israelites did, and not stop at the shoreline. We can and will follow on so others may follow.

As a woman minister, I know how nasty the attacks can be and how ugly words can be, but they are nothing in comparison to walking in the Truth and Promises of God. Jesus is the Way, the Truth, and the Life.

My Reflections *Date*_____

❧❧ 87 ❧❧

Half-Truths and White Lies

> The Lord God commanded the man, saying, "From any tree of the garden you may eat freely; but from the tree of the knowledge of good and evil you shall not eat, for in the day that you eat from it you will surely die" (Genesis 2:16-17).

> The woman said to the serpent, "From the fruit of the trees of the garden we may eat; but from the fruit of the tree which is in the middle of the garden, God has said, 'You shall not eat from it or touch it, or you will die'" (Genesis 3:2-3).

God said not to eat of the tree. Somehow, Eve was given to understand that she was not even to touch the tree. She had been told a half-truth or a *harmless, white lie.* When she touched the fruit, and nothing happened, she went on to eat of the fruit. So, the half-truth opened the door for the enemy to enter the Garden. As the Lord was showing this to me, I could see how this illustrates a progression that often happens.

Half-truths are dangerous! How much adultery starts with a half-truth or a white lie? How many uses of drugs—legal and illegal—start with a half-truth or a white lie? How many betrayals? How many thefts?

Now, think about how half-truths or white lies are told about God. For example, if you do this, God is going to get you! Then, when the act is carried out without apparent consequences, that person might throw out what is, in fact, true.

I often hear someone dismiss a wrong by saying, "It was only a little white lie," or "I only told them half the truth, so it is okay." But is it? Something to think on, isn't it?

My Reflections   *Date*_____

❧❧ 88 ❧❧

What Is the Gospel Truth?

> The one who says, "I have come to know Him," and does not keep His commandments, is a liar, and the truth is not in him; but whoever keeps His word, in him the love of God has truly been perfected. By this we know that we are in Him: the one who says he abides in Him ought himself to walk in the same manner as He walked (1 John 2:4-6).

This has been an interesting week at the office. One of my tasks is to handle complaints, and this week, I had a person bring a complaint to me. Over and over, this person said, "This is the gospel truth! It is no lie!"

I have heard people say this before, but this time, the Lord had me really hear it! As a result, when this statement is made, I question what *gospel* are they referring to?

The people who come to me with complaints know that I am a Christian and that I love the Word of God. So, what did God want me to see in this statement? The answer, I believe, is the need for those who have some knowledge of the Word to have a greater revelation of what God's Word really says and to walk in it—not as works, but out of God's love and righteousness. In other words, this person needs the Ephesians prayers prayed on their behalf!

My Reflections   *Date*_____

89

Not Ashamed of the Gospel

For I am not ashamed of the gospel, for it is the power of God for salvation to everyone who believes, to the Jew first and also to the Greek (Romans 1:16).

I am not ashamed of the Gospel of Jesus Christ! I know Jesus is my Lord and Savior. I know I have been created in the image of God, my Creator. I know the precious Holy Spirit dwells within me. So, what keeps me from sharing this wonderful truth more often? Fear! Fear of failure. Fear of rejection. Fear of not saying things exactly right.

But God has not given us a spirit of fear, but a spirit of love, of power, and of a sound, disciplined mind (2 Timothy 1:7). When it dawns on us that God's power released to us and through us as we tell others about Him and His truth, we are no longer subject to fear.

When what we are sharing is what we are living, we want others to know the salvation and presence of Almighty God in their own lives. Our heart is for people to know the love of God for themselves.

My Reflections   *Date*_____

❧❧ 90 ❧❧

Acknowledge God

**Pride goes before destruction,
And a haughty spirit before stumbling
(Proverbs 16:18)**

Pride is not a good thing! The devil got kicked out of Heaven because of pride. It causes people to see things in a false light. It makes them think they are doing things in their own power and they begin to think more highly of themselves than they ought. If we aren't careful to give God glory and to thank Him, we will find ourselves in a dangerous place, with pride lurking to take over.

I can tell you that I do a good job and always give my best, yet when I make a mistake, I realize that I can't do any of this alone. I must have God's help all the way, all the time—even in the routine things of life.

When we lack knowledge, the Holy Spirit will give us the insight we need—if we are listening! But when we are doing it on our own, we won't hear the Spirit's leadings. Proverbs 3:5-6 provides wise counsel.

*Trust in the Lord with all your heart
And do not lean on your own understanding.
In all your ways acknowledge Him,
And He will make your paths straight.*

My Reflections   *Date*_____

About the Author

Susan Osborn Schultz is an ordained minister of the Gospel of Jesus Christ. She is a wife, mother, grandmother, and great grandmother.

She holds a Bachelor's degree in Biblical Studies from the International School of Ministry, and a Christian Life Coach Certificate from Professional Christian Coaching and Counseling Academy. She is also a graduate of Word of Faith Bible School.

Susan has been active in many facets of ministry for over 35 years. She is on the Advisory Board of God's Word to Women, Inc., The Int'l Christian Women's Hall of Fame, and The Spirit of the Lord's Ministry. She is part of the faculty of God's Word to the World College and its Christian Women's Studies Program, and has taught on KSHY Radio. Susan has served as Associate Pastor in two different churches and has worked with four senior pastors.

From 2003 until 2015, she was the Academic Dean of Cheyenne Bible Training Center, and in 2014, she established Laramie Bible Training Center. Susan has served on the Board of Directors of Northern Colorado Christians for Biblical Equality and various Aglow chapters in Wyoming, Nebraska, and South Dakota. She organized Cheyenne's *March for Jesus* for three years.

Susan's heart is for people to know Jesus and the Word of God. In this devotional book, she shares her life experiences to encourage the reader to know that God loves them, that God is for them, and that they can be free of bondage and walk in victory.

✎✎ How to Contact Susan ✎✎

If this devotional book has helped you, Susan would love to hear from you.

We invite you to read more devotionals at Susan's devotional blog: godswordtowomentoday.blogspot.com

She is available to minister in your fellowship, home group, seminar, conference, Bible school, or church.

Mailing Address
Susan Osborn Schultz
P. O. Box 3425
Gilbert, AZ 85299

Internet Addresses
Email: SusanOsbornSchultz@gmail.com
FaceBook: Susan Schultz

Made in the USA
San Bernardino, CA
22 August 2019